LEAVING *the* DARK HOUSE

A true story of survival by

LAURA M. FROMBACH

I have tried to recreate events, locales and conversations from my memories of them. In order to maintain their anonymity in some instances I have changed the names of individuals and places, I may have changed some identifying characteristics and details such as physical properties, occupations and places of residence.

Credits
Book cover design and interior layout by
Ellie Bockert Augsburger of Creative Digital Studios.
Editing by Carl Augsburger of Creative Digital Studios.
www.CreativeDigitalStudios.com

Cover Design Images
Out there: © Olexandr / Dollar Photo Club
Butterfly Orange Isolates: © pupes1 / Dollar Photo Club

FOREWORD

The odds of someone who grew up like I did winding up as a regular person are nil. This is the story of a broken family made up of shattered people. The brokenness had been ongoing for generations, each one successively crushing their children with abuse and trauma. Although this story relates my family's generational brokenness in the extreme, remember that we are all damaged to some degree.

As Hemingway noted, "The world breaks everyone and afterward many are strong in the broken places." Every one of us has had a piece chipped off of our soul in some regard...some pieces are just bigger than others. If you think that you can never retrieve that part of you or put the fragmented pieces back together again, this story is for you. Despite the odds, I am stronger in the broken places. If I can do it, anyone can, even you. The odds only matter if you're playing the odds.

To
Teri Bunetta, M.Ed, LMHC
Steven N. Gold, PH.D
And always, for Joy

We shall crush you down to the point from which there is no coming back. Things will happen to you from which you could not recover, if you lived a thousand years. Never again will you be capable of ordinary human feeling. Everything will be dead inside you. Never again will you be capable of love, or friendship, or joy of living, or laughter, or curiosity, or courage, or integrity. You will be hollow. We shall squeeze you empty and then we shall fill you with ourselves.

-GEORGE ORWELL, *1984*

It is not having been in the Dark House, but having left it, that counts.

-THEODORE ROOSEVELT

CHAPTER ONE

1966

The Imp was on the hunt. There was no indication that you or anyone else who didn't know the game would recognize. There was no sound or anything else obviously amiss. But I sensed it. I knew. I could feel the charge in the air. All prey knows when the hunter is afoot. It was only a matter of time until I was found. I had no thought of fleeing. It wouldn't have done any good; there was no escape. It would end badly. It always did. But I wasn't afraid. Honest, I wasn't. If I'd been allowed to swear without getting my mouth washed out with Fels Naptha soap, I would have said that I was pissed, pissed off and tired. Weary of the endless cat-and-mouse games, I wanted them to end. I just wanted some peace. I hated the Imp. I would kill it if I could.

Although furious, I still made a pathetic attempt to hide. I was angry, not stupid. If prey can't flee, it holes up. It doesn't flag down the predator to lodge a complaint. Hunkered down into the mattress of the top bunk in the small bedroom that I shared with my younger sister, I tried to pretend that I wasn't there. Ok, maybe I was a little scared, if truth were told. It wasn't anything that I couldn't manage, though. I'd handled worse.

Head resting on my hands, I listened intently, waiting for the bedroom door to open any moment. With my freckled face and lopsided brown hair, I resembled *To Kill a Mockingbird's* Scout Finch with a bad haircut. I was small for my age and scrawny, even for an eleven year old. I hoped that I was so small that I couldn't be seen under the covers. Tiny swells of fear began to wash over the seawall of my anger. As the minutes ticked by, the waves got larger, threatening to crush the seawall into pieces. Soon, the rage would be completely swallowed into a black sea of terror, leaving only acrid and debilitating dread in its wake. I'd be rendered powerless by own weakness.

I hated being afraid even more than I hated the Imp. Fear is the first symptom of weakness. I needed to toughen up for what I knew would lie ahead. I needed a show of strength. Angry people are strong, unlike fraidy cats. Despite my resolve, my hands began to tremble. I'd covered myself with the pale pink sheet and thick blue blanket, and I gripped the flowered bottom sheet to stop my hands from shaking. The Imp would sense the weakness of fear and feed off of it.

Until the moment that I'd sensed the Imp, I'd been re-reading a 1945 volume of the Book of Knowledge encyclopedia for the umpteenth time. Like Scout, I was also a tomboy and voracious bookworm, devouring anything in print. I perused cereal boxes at breakfast if nothing else was available. It drove my parents insane. Barely literate themselves and unburdened by any form of curiosity, my parents couldn't comprehend my obsession. But if I could find something to read that didn't cost anything, then it was all the same to them. The only thing that I enjoyed besides reading was raising Monarch butterflies. I'd find the yellow and black caterpillars on stalks of milkweed and keep them in large jars, changing their milkweed every day until they turned into small, green chrysalises. A couple of weeks later, beautiful orange and black butterflies would emerge and I'd let them go after their wings had dried. I often pretended that I could ride the Monarchs like a getaway horse to some magical land far away.

When I was a very little girl, my father took me on weekly trips to the library where I'd stack up as many books as I could carry. But those days were long gone. They were as lost as many of the normal things that we used to do. It seemed as though we had been like everyone else at one time. I sometimes remembered when the family used to enjoy watching *The Munsters* in front of the TV together. But by my eleventh year, we hadn't laughed with Herman and Lily for a long time. Our small black and white television with the bent hanger antenna had either finally answered its last call, or my father had smashed it in one of his drunken tirades. It no longer mattered.

As I read through the faded blue encyclopedia with its slightly yellowed pages, I momentarily considered where my siblings might be. As the oldest, I was hardwired to want to know their whereabouts at all times. My two younger sisters were probably playing across the street at the neighbor's house to pass the time on this cold winter's Saturday. All of us always went out. It was an unspoken rule that no one came *in* to our house to play; all of us kids knew better. You would never know when a dinner plate (or your face) could go flying against the wall. That wasn't the type of party trick that one showed off for friends. We looked for any excuse to get out of the house, even requesting sleepovers as gifts. When my grandmother or aunt would ask for birthday or holiday requests, we would tell that them we really didn't want anything, but could we spend the weekend at their house? Any respite was welcome.

While my siblings could usually be found out playing with their friends, I was usually at home. Shy and acutely conscious of my cat-eye glasses and my mother's homemade haircut, I was socially awkward and had few friends. My sister Beth would occasionally invite me to go with her and her pals, but these invitations were infrequent, as she had more fun without her bossy older sister. Who cared? I preferred reading to their pointless childish games anyway.

I knew that hoping to avoid detection was futile...it was as pointless as spitting into a tempest. It wasn't as though I was playing hide and seek with the royals in Buckingham Palace and could hope to get lost in a large mansion or hide in the crowd of butlers and ladies-in-waiting. Cinderella had left this building with the prince, and I had inherited her cinderous accommodations along with her ill-tempered family. The bedroom that I shared with my sister Beth was just large enough to contain bunk beds, an old dresser, and a small table. The tiny table could just accommodate an ancient 45rpm record player. I thought sarcastically that the small sound system was old enough to be an original Edison. Even my mother's homemade curtains were a tight fit in the tiny room. However, the curtains that Gertie's sewing machine turned out had a much better outcome than the coifs that her scissors provided for her children.

There were no pre-teen posters of the Beatles on the walls, although a few worn Tiger Beat magazines were squirreled away in the closet. My parents considered such indulgences trash, ostensibly igniting our pre-pubescent hormones. No wonder the TV had never been replaced. If it had, perhaps we would have someday been driven into a hormonal frenzy to find ourselves inexplicably throwing our giraffe underwear at the television when Ed Sullivan featured the Rolling Stones playing *Let's Spend Some Time Together*. Taking no chances on raising early grandchildren or letting the outside world otherwise intrude, no information was leaked into or outside of our family. Mum's the word in an alcoholic home.

Our munchkin-sized bedroom was proportionate to the teeny three-bedroom flat rented from my mother's cousin. It was cheap, but free of vermin and insects – something that couldn't be said of all of my relative's homes. Our family squeezed into the bottom unit of a 60-year-old house; a size-four apartment for a size-eight family. We'd gotten the zipper up with some help, but the seams definitely groaned and the threads could be seen. My parents slept in the master bedroom, which barely accommodated the double bed and dresser that they couldn't have afforded if the set hadn't been a wedding gift. Beth and I shared the middle room with the wagon-wheel bunk beds, while my younger sister slept in a third bedroom that was no bigger than a closet. Even her dresser sat in the hallway. The only wall decorations anywhere in the apartment were pictures of Baby Jesus and His Blessed Mother on small hook rugs that my aunt had made for my mother.

The apartment was cluttered but fairly clean, as my mother's children were not permitted to do anything on Saturday morning until the house had been dusted and vacuumed and the floors had been damp-mopped. The couch was used as a makeshift linen closet, holding a permanent pile of towels. The towels had originally been placed there in the hopes that some passerby would immediately note that they needed to be folded and take care of it in about 10 minutes. Instead, we all took to grabbing a towel out of the pile when needed and pushing the pile from one side of the couch to the other when we wanted a seat. On those rare occasions when company was expected, the pile magically disappeared into the mountainous permanent laundry pile in the basement, only to just as wondrously reappear the next day.

In addition to the bedrooms, the rest of the apartment left little to the imagination. The mustard-yellow walls looked as though they were exhausted from holding the house up for all those years. The walls overlooked a porous cork floor that never quite looked clean. A dining room housed the "formal" company dining table as well as my mother's sewing machine, and the living room was cleverly decorated with three layers of carpets so that each one hid the bare spots of the others. This was a house plan that definitely favored the seeker in my reluctant game of hide-and-seek.

I slowly raised my head away from mismatched sheets to see if the coast was clear for a moment. I would be momentarily exposed, but hoped to ultimately improve my chances of concealment. I quickly whisked the two decrepit bed pillows to the side of the bunk facing the door. I felt like a prison inmate rehearsing for the great escape, hoping against hope that the pillows would hide my small frame. I thought that maybe the Imp would somehow confuse human with bedclothes. But a good hunter laughs at camouflage, and I knew the Imp would get a good chuckle. I burrowed back down behind the pillows, pushing myself as far into the mattress as I could go. To distract myself from my terror, I mentally reviewed some of the information revealed by the ancient encyclopedia. I recalled such valuable information as diamond mining methodologies in South Africa, and then skipped ahead to silently reciting different breeds of dairy cows. My awareness continued to probe the silence as I awaited the inevitable.

Although I tried to calm myself by staying focused on the riveting encyclopedia information, my terror spiked. I berated myself again for my weakness and silently prayed to Baby Jesus and His Blessed Mother with the fervor of a foxhole convert. "Please,

Baby Jesus, spirit me away and bring me to home to heaven with you."

I had hopes of being a nun when I was old enough, and tried to be scholar of the Bible (when not engrossed in aged encyclopedias). I was also the number-one fan of the *Lives of the Saints* collection, volumes one through four. Fortunately, it didn't occur to me at the time that no saint story ever ended with happily-ever-after, or I would have been even more depressed than I already was.

Jesus' generosity with loaves and fishes for the masses, the ever popular water-into-wine party trick, and walking on stormy seas to save his people seemed to come to an abrupt halt when he changed zip codes from Galilee to Heaven. He made two more quick trips after His trading-up Ascension: once with his Holy Spirit pal to give a pep talk to his disciples, and then a solo visit to give Saul a well-deserved smack upside the head. After providing the newly chastened Paul with a name makeover and a sorely needed Gentile marketing boost, Jesus made the final exit back up to His new digs. Unfortunately, there have been a lot of people since Saul/Paul who've needed a good heavenly swat and have gotten away swat-free. The saints had been on their own, and so was I.

I finally heard it. Had I not been listening so intently, I might have missed the sound of the door handle as it quietly turned. Bit by bit, the handle slowly rotated. It seemed to take an eternity, although in reality, it probably took no more than a few seconds. My breath caught. An ever so slight squeal from old hinges announced that the door was moving. The aged hinges needed attention, as did everything else in our house. The door barely opened before it stopped.

A low giggle emitted from the newly created crack between the frame and the door. A childish, sing-song voice emanated from the mouth pressed up against the crack. "Sissy Lors, are you there?"

Through the tiny space between door and frame, I could faintly hear the instrumental version of Simon and Garfunkel's *I am a Rock* floating through the apartment. The old table radio incessantly puked Muzak in the kitchen. No "jungle music" (as my mother called rock-and-roll), was allowed to accidentally incite a hormonal flare-up.

Forehead deep into the mattress, I exhaled without moving. My eyes squinted shut. Motionless, I continued to silently pray. I'd given up on Jesus, but held out a sliver of hope that His Blessed Mother might still be paying attention and would put in a good word to her son...a practice not unlike telling someone's mother on them when you really want to get their attention. I sent out a mental SOS to the Blessed Mother, hoping flattery would work.

"Hail, Holy Queen, Mother of Mercy, our life, our sweetness, and our hope. To thee do we cry, poor banished children of Eve. To thee do we send up our sighs, mourning and weeping in this valley of tears." I hoped that she'd get a move on and beat feet with some help. There were about 3 grains of sand left in the hourglass.

Fuck it. I prayer-dialed Jesus again. "Please, Jesus. Please. I'll be good. I'll be good. I'll be good," I chanted quietly.

Thoughts screamed inside my head like the panic sirens on a ship. "Help me. Help. Jesus! Can't you do ANY goddamn THING? Jesus goddamn Christ!" The hinges complained again as the door opened another inch or so and held.

"Sissy Lors, hi! I know that you're here. Come and play with me. I want to play! I see you! Peek-a-boo! No hiding! Come play with me! Let's play!"

I gripped the sheet a little tighter over my head, futilely hoping that the Imp would think that I was napping – not that it would matter. All that mattered to the Imp was what the Imp wanted. Finally, the door flung open and bounced off of the wall. The laughing Imp, in stocking feet, covered the distance between the door and the bunk in two steps and leapt up onto the bunk ladder. My pathetic bed fort went flying.

"Go away. I'm sleeping," I mumbled, doing my best imitation of groggy. I refused to look up, holding the decrepit pillow over my head, a pitiful shield. I felt bouncing as the Imp jumped up and down on the ladder like a maniacal Chucky. The pillow was pulled out of my hands. I felt hot breath in my face, smelling of braunschweiger and onions on rye.

"No, you're not! You're awake! Ha ha! I see you!"

The Imp playfully pulled my hair and I gave a swat, hitting air. I felt another hair tug. Harder, this time it hurt. "Sissy Lors! It is time for you to play with me!" The next hair pull hurt like hell.

"Leave me alone! I'm trying to sleep. I'll play with you later, I promise." The Imp would have none of my empty bullshit. Four knuckles hit my face as the backhand hit home. Practiced. Not hard, but no love tap.

My eyes popped open immediately and I shot up, spring-loaded. Cheek red with the blow and redder with rage, I moved fast, but the Imp was faster. Giggling and leaping to the floor with glee, the Imp bounced up and down, a jack-in-the-box without a home. I bypassed the bunk ladder and jumped to the floor. No carpeting cushioned my landing on the bare linoleum, but I didn't feel a thing. I was so enraged that I could have plummeted 10 stories and not felt it. Her thin, fine hair askew like a mad scarecrow, the Imp's long, skinny hand came in as a blur for another direct hit. The solid blow across my cheek was infuriating, but not hard enough to bruise.

"That's it, I've had it!" I screamed at the laughing face. I went in to return the favor of the face slap, but the Imp danced out of the way and assumed a practiced defense stance. Giggling demonically, the Imp taunted me.

"Sissy Lors! Play, play, play! Let's play!"

I went in for another try and received a rough shoulder push, enough to fuel my rage but not enough to make me lose my balance. The battle was on. The Imp continued taunting, pushing, and slapping. I landed a blow every now and then, but I was way out of my league and I knew it. I was a rank amateur against a world-class champ. The Imp had several distinct advantages: skill, speed, and the absence of blind rage. I knew better than to call or yell for assistance; no one else was home. Besides, I knew that my sisters were no match for this hound from hell. It was up to me. It was always up to me. I was the only one who could engage the Imp, because I had a secret weapon.

We continued our strange dance down the hallway, almost knocking over my sister's dresser that inexplicably held my grandfather's broken old typewriter. There was no other place in the flat for the dresser, but the presence of the typewriter was a mystery. Most of the keys didn't work, yet it had remained there for years. It was as odd as everything else in our lives.

Through the kitchen to the dining room we lurched, poking and slapping. Despite the Imp's laughing and giggling, I could sense an underlying, inexplicable anger. In the open space near the sewing machine, I made a mad lunge. Anticipating the move, the Imp quickly back stepped and hooked a foot behind my ankle. The Imp pulled my foot forward and I fell back, my head bouncing on the braided rug. I gasped for breath, the wind knocked out of me.

Triumphant, the Imp sneered. "Not quite quick enough. Are you, sis?"

Immediately, I felt the Imp's bony claws pinning down my shoulders. The cackling wolfish face was suddenly inches from my own, taunting me to get up, so close that everything else was obstructed from my range of view. There was no escape and we both knew it. Vision red with rage, I pressed back into the floor, then suddenly threw my head up and slammed my head into the Imp's forehead as hard as I could.

The Imp's taunting face turned immediately to ice and she gave me a backhand. "You little witch. I'll teach you to control that temper. I was just having a little fun and now you've ruined it." Backing off warily to avoid another head slam, the Imp shoved a narrow finger in the soft spot directly under my nose and applied pressure, hard enough to keep my head immobile. The next thing I knew, my shoulders were pinned under the Imp's knees. Slap. Slap. Slap. The Imp whacked my face back and forth several times. The smacks weren't hard enough to leave a mark, just enough to swat my head from one side to the other as though I were watching an invisible tennis match.

"How do you like them apples? Huh, sis? This will teach you. You'll control that temper one way or the other." Slap. Slap.

"Stop it! Stop it!" I finally broke.

Slap. Slap.

Sobbing, I tried to spit, but the Imp was too far away. I wound up spitting on my own shirt. I bucked like a possessed bronco, but was outmatched and I knew it. Eventually I must have zoned out, because I completely lost track of time. I had no idea how much longer the game went on. Finally, the Imp tired of it and I felt the pressure released from my shoulders as her bony knees were removed. But I still couldn't budge, as the scrawny forefinger had returned to the soft spot on top of my front teeth. The pressure effectively paralyzed me until I was dragged off the floor by the front of my t-shirt. From previous battles, I knew what was coming. If I had fought like a bronco to eject the Imp off of me, it was nothing compared to my thrashing and flailing now. I felt like the damned at the mouth of hell. Lashing and bucking, I grabbed the door frame with both hands until the Imp peeled my fingers away. From experience, I knew better than to scream, as that would just guarantee a fist jammed deep into my mouth. Pure panic, twisting, spitting, clawing, I felt like a doomed animal at the slaughterhouse door. I fought the inevitable. The trip to the bathroom was short, fifteen feet at best. Even with the strength of my rage, I was no match for the Imp. She dragged my spastic body into the bathtub; applying pressure to the soft spot with one hand and turning the cold water full blast with the other.

Human beings don't have an infinite amount of energy, and rage burns through the body's resources like the fire that it is. As the tub filled with icy liquid, I slowly, finally, reluctantly gave up the fight and went limp, submerged into what felt like a dark arctic prison. I was numb in body and spirit. The Imp held me down into the frigid water until she was certain that I had given up, and said grimly through thin lips, "This will cool down that anger problem that you have, young lady. I just wanted to play, and you ruined it like you always do. You'd better learn to control that temper, sis, or I'll control it for you."

Like a cat that finally tires of the game long after the mouse has expired, the Imp had played enough for one day and I was too exhausted to cry any more. We went our separate ways in the small flat. I knew from experience that my mother's game was over for the day. She was celebrating her victory with a cigarette. I wondered if no-show Jesus and Mary were watching from heaven. The hell with them. My secret weapon had finally kicked in and I magicked my mind away. My body was soaked and shivering, but me...I was a million miles away.

By now you may be thinking: "Hey, kid. If you knew your old lady was out to get you, why didn't you just leave the house? You could have even crawled out of a window or something, for crying out loud. What's wrong with you? You couldn't have been all that smart, reading all of those encyclopedias or not." And, under normal circumstances, I would wholeheartedly agree with you. Any prey that knows the predator is nearby and hides in a stupid bed fort instead of getting the hell out of there is definitely one big dope. A big dope that will soon have more trouble than she can handle.

This wasn't this big dope's first rodeo. My mother had been playing her little game for a long time. By then, it was hard to tell exactly how long it had been going on, maybe a year or more. But I knew from experience that when the Imp was about, she would get someone. Anyone. The Imp needed someone to break, and she wasn't going to stop until they were broken and crying...and the only toys that she had to break were her children. I knew that if my mother didn't play her Imp game with me, she would have played it with Beth or Mary Pat. She was like a car running on empty: when you need a fill up, any gas station will do.

I couldn't let her do that to my siblings for a couple of reasons. First of all, I'm a big sister and we're territorial beasts. We can terrorize our siblings, but no one else can, including our parents. We're somehow hard-wired to protect them, even when we really don't feel like it. But there was also something else, a secret that only I knew about. It was the secret that had kept me in that house when anyone with an ounce of common sense would have gotten out. It wasn't because I was a big dope, nor was I a docile martyr, willing to be complicit in a fight that I knew was unwinnable. The main reason that I baited myself in that trap in the bunk bed was that I knew that my sisters didn't have my special power. They couldn't make themselves separate from their body the way that I could. I could be here one minute and gone the next, so I knew that I could take anything that the Imp could dish out.

Many children of violence have to develop special powers. The moods of volatile parents flash in an instant and their children develop early warning systems that would rival anything that NORAD could invent, even if they had an unlimited budget and hundreds of years to work. We have to, our lives and sanity depends on it. The slightest altering of any behavior is foreboding; a flickering glance imperceptible to the untrained eye, a slight flare of the nostrils and a deep breath, a purse of the lips, a longer silence than normal. We might not register the signs consciously, but we sure as hell come to attention when our internal warning siren shrills. I never discussed my parents' poker tells with my siblings, but their sirens must have silently blared as well because they'd suddenly fade out of sight like ghosts. They were smart, and I couldn't blame them one little bit. If I hadn't developed my special powers, I would have been the first one out of the door.

CHAPTER TWO

1953

The one thing that the relatives could agree on about my parents was that they had started out well. In fact, they'd seemed to be the perfect couple. They'd met on a blind date that Aunt Kay had arranged. Gertie Kalvelage had been eighteen, just out of high school and somewhat shy in those days. Attractive in her own way, the high school pictures of my mother showed a strong resemblance to Jamie Lee Curtis. She spent a lot of time curling her hair with bobby pins every night and wore just enough makeup to be considered pretty. Her wardrobe tended toward size eight J.C. Penny and Sears Roebuck dresses or pedal pushers (as capris were known in those days), light on the jewelry; she was an early June Cleaver in search of her Ward.

She hadn't dated much, but her older sister knew just the guy to liven her up: Wild Bill Frombach. Aunt Kay and Wild Bill ran with same crowd, a little rowdy and always having fun. Bill was a live wire who could always be counted on to bring the party. Quick with a joke and a grin, he was good looking in a Perry Como sort of way, and he fancied himself a ladies' man. Having been around the block a time or two, he used all of his smooth moves on Gertie and immediately swept her off her feet. She was crazy about this handsome, fun guy and fell madly in love. She later said that he was the funniest and nicest guy that she'd ever met.

Gert and Kay's parents weren't quite as infatuated with Billy Boy. Their daughter was definitely smitten, but he was hardly husband material in their eyes. They were glad that Gertie was happy, but they'd had higher hopes for a serious relationship. Not only was Wild Bill just a grocery boy, but he also had a wide crude streak and bragged of his ability to drink anyone under the table. My grandmother said many rosaries and novenas that he would move on or that Gertie would meet someone else. Eventually Uncle Sam heard her prayers and sent Wild Bill his draft notice. He soon left for Germany to cook for the troops, and my grandparents were certain that time and distance would put a damper on their daughter's puppy love. They sent Aunt Kay back out on the hunt, and she brought several prospects to distract her lovesick sister. But Gertie wasn't interested, she'd found her man. She spent the next two years wrapped up in a romantic fantasy with the prince of her dreams. My mother wrote long love letters every day and slept by the phone every night, hoping for his call. Unsurprisingly, they became engaged as soon as Billy Boy was discharged. The relatives said that they'd never seen a happier couple. Even her parents finally relented and had to admit that not only had Wild Bill brought Gertie out of her shell, but he didn't seem quite so wild around her. Maybe this would work out after all.

After they announced their engagement, Wild Bill took his fiancée out to meet his father. My grandmother had died when Bill was two, and the old man had never remarried. He still lived on the farm that he'd had since he came over from the old country. Bill's father was an immigrant, having arrived in the United States from Transylvania right before WWI, narrowly avoiding conscription into the Kaiser's Army. At the time, Transylvania was still under Austro-Hungarian rule, and Bill's family forever considered themselves proud Austrians. After 40 years in America, the old man still spoke with a heavy German accent. He shared many traits with another native Transylvanian: Vlad the Impaler. Known for his extreme brutality and cruelty, Vlad was the basis for Bram Stoker's Dracula. My grandfather was the polar opposite of his happy-go-lucky son. Toughened by life and made strong by many years as a farmer, Matthias Frombach was a thick, powerful man with curly white hair. In my parents' wedding picture, he looked like he had just walked out of the fields wearing a borrowed suit and had ducked into the bathroom to slick back his hair. Face hardened into a permanent scowl and character hardened by permanent rage, he terrorized his children and almost everyone else he encountered.

Shortly after arriving in the U.S., Matthias met and married my grandmother and immediately got and kept her pregnant. Like many women of that era, she died in childbirth after pumping out eight children amidst several miscarriages. One could argue that she didn't die, she escaped. After the death of his wife in 1934, Matthias attempted to raise his eight children alone on a remote farm outside of tiny Albion, PA. But Matthias was challenged by conflicting priorities. A baker by trade, he left the farm every morning at 3:00 a.m. to travel 25 miles to his job in the city. After working long hours, he came home exhausted, interrupting his drinking only long enough to raise the crops necessary to feed his brood. When it got dark and he could no longer see to plow or harvest, he would drink himself from blind rage into oblivion, then rise the next morning to begin the process all over again. In his long to-do list, his children typically never made it above the last line. He tried to make up for it by beating the hell out of each of them on a regular basis. Still, they were left to their own devices most of the time, so they terrorized each other and the neighboring farms. Unfortunately, there was no nearby abbey where my grandfather could order up a Maria Von Trapp to amuse the children by day and keep him happy by night. He was a lonely goatherd indeed.

Matthias was relieved of his parental obligations by the state of Pennsylvania when my uncles burned the barn down. It was almost certainly not the first family prank that the authorities had been called for, and most assuredly was not the last time that the state would intervene in the lives of my relatives. The male children who were old enough joined the Navy, while the rest of the clan was sent to St. Joseph's orphanage. This was where Bill spent most of his childhood. A kind woman named Mrs. King fostered Bill and three of his siblings when he was around twelve years old. Mrs. King was the only mother that Bill had ever known, and she did her best to be a good mother to them. Wild Bill attributed everything good about himself to Mrs. King and worshipped her to the day she died.

We would occasionally visit my grandfather when I was a young child, and I learned to dread the visits. Unlike my mother's parents, Mimi and Bumpy, who could be sharp with their children but worshipped their grandchildren, Grandpy was unpredictable and mean with everyone. He scared me. Grandpy worked at the bakery into his sixties, and we were sometimes surprised to find a large bucket of day-old donuts waiting for us when we arrived at his house. Holding the tempting container of sticky, gooey, delectable snacks in front of us so that we could smell them, he kept them just out of reach. My cousins and I could see dozens of powdery cinnamon and jelly treats. The sight of so many tasty goodies in one place was almost too overwhelming for a child to behold, but we weren't going to get them quite so easily.

"Do you vant a donut? Look at dem! Don't dey look vonderful? You surely vant a donut!" he bellowed at us in his thick accent. He waved the bucket of sugary delights in front of us, just inches from outstretched fingers.

We certainly did vant one! We were so lucky that our grandfather was a baker! A whole bucket of donuts! Jumping up and down at the prospect, we squealed and reached toward the container with small hands. "Yes, Grandpy! Yes, please!" we cried. He would taunt us with the donuts before finally allowing us to have them.

I had mixed feelings about those donuts. I was terrified of getting so close to the mean old man, but just couldn't resist the magnetic pull of the pastries. Then one day, my confusion was settled for good, on the day that Grandpy's true character came out. That day, Grandpy pulled the container back suddenly and said, "Ach, no. Not quite yet, kinder. You must haff sandvich first."

Grandpy's eyes burned bright, his odd smile demonstrating his complete disregard for dental hygiene. "Vonce you haff sandwich, you may haff donut – maybe two donut if you eat all of sandwich! You vant sandwich now?"

Like Pavlov's dogs, we salivated at the sight and smell of the delicacies so close and yet so far away. We would have promised anything. A sandwich was a small price to pay for admittance to the heavenly bucket. Besides, our parents would have made the same bargain with us. Lunch first, then dessert.

"Vunderbar!" my grandfather's voice boomed. "Go houtside and I make you sandwich. Once sandwich finished, then donuts!"

We ran outside to the rotting wooden picnic table that had more than likely been languishing since my father lived there. Grampy didn't make us wait long, and shortly arrived outside balancing several sandwiches on paper plates. Almost dancing with excitement, we grabbed the sandwiches as soon as he put them down and eagerly took a large bite. My grandfather stared at us intently, awaiting our reaction. We immediately spit out the bread, onion, horseradish, and bitter limburger cheese, breaking into sobs.

Grampy's laughter boomed as he said, "Vhat? No sandwich? You don't like sandwich? Such spoiled children. No sandvich, no donut!"

On a bright August afternoon, my father pulled up to the old homestead with his fiancée in his brother-in-law's black hardtop Nash Rambler that he'd borrowed just for the occasion. His own Plymouth beater was fine for banging around town, but as he would put it years later when telling the story, he was afraid that it would "shit the bed" if pushed for the thirty-mile drive to the farm. The young couple enjoyed listening to the radio, and Dean Martin was singing *That's Amore* as the car rolled to a stop in the dusty driveway. Bill commented to Gertie that he'd probably have to wash the car before he returned it – his brother-in-law would have a fit if it came back with gritty dirt on its shiny surface. The comment was more of a pragmatic observation than pride in the auto's appearance. Uncle Al loved his cars and babied them. Parking a dusty car in Al's driveway would guarantee that Bill would be up the creek the next time he needed a loaner for a long drive.

A couple of quick toots on the horn announced their arrival. Matthias had no phone, so there was no way of letting him know that they were on the way. It would have been an unnecessary call anyway; the only reason that Grampy ever left the farm was to go to work. Dressed in their nicest outfits and Sunday best shoes for the occasion, Bill kept an eye on the front door as he waited patiently for

Gertie to freshen her pale pink lipstick in the rearview mirror. The old man usually came out when he heard the horn, but this time the door remained still.

Wild Bill was uncharacteristically nervous and a little embarrassed. He'd never brought anyone to meet his father before. His fiancée was what he liked to call a classy dame, and the farm wasn't the place for a gal with class. He grabbed a quick nip of liquid courage from the bottle that he had stashed under the front seat. The perspiration running down his neck mixed with the Old Spice cologne that he'd slapped on just before leaving his sister's house. As the lipstick returned to Gertie's clutch, he ran around the car and opened the passenger door for her. He grabbed her hand and gave her a reassuring grin as they approached the wooden farmhouse. He opened the screen door and called out, "Yoo-hoo! Anyone home? I brought a surprise!"

He was greeted by silence.

Bill went in first and pulled his fiancée in behind him. Gertie said later that he'd kept a tight grip on her so that she couldn't take off once she saw what was inside. The inside of the farmhouse looked like a bomb had exploded during the war and people had continued to live their lives around the rubble. Paint and sanitation had been abandoned long ago. Thousands of flies made their home there, disgusting offspring from a convenient marriage of open windows and rotting food. The place smelled horrific. Every time my mother told the story, she'd add that the stench was enough to gag a maggot. I had to agree, as the stink never lessened over the years. From visiting the old man, I acquired the handy skill of learning to breathe without smelling. It's easy, just focus on breathing through your mouth. At the time, Gertie had to press the inside of her wrist against her nose; it was perhaps the only time that anyone had to depend on the power of Estee Lauder to prevent them from gagging. Accustomed to the malodor and domestic disaster, my father forged ahead, dragging his fiancée through the filth on his hunt for the old German.

Stopping at the bedroom, they ensured that it was vacant as well. My mother got a glimpse of an unmade metal-framed bed with grey, filthy sheets. Grungy clothes were strewn over every inch of the floor, making it look like a detonated thrift store. An empty Old Crow bottle lay on a heap of pants left where he'd dropped them beside the nightstand. Years later, one of my aunts said that their father had taken to keeping a bottle under the bed so he wouldn't have to endure sobriety for long after waking. After he had his morning fix, he would then fill his ever-present hip flask to ensure a consistent blood alcohol level throughout the day.

Doubling back through the living room, they headed to the back door. Still dragging my mother, Bill barely glanced at the back stoop littered with empty whiskey bottles strewn everywhere. He continued toward the barn, which my grandfather had single-handedly rebuilt after his sons had burned it down years ago. Wild Bill led his fiancée into the building. As the couple walked further into the darkened barn and their eyes adjusted to the dim light, they felt their shoes sinking into the muck, enveloped by a swamp of cow manure. Gertie held back tears as the ammonia of cow urine assaulted her senses and the week's salary that she'd spent on those shoes flew out the barn door. Neither Grampy nor bovine were anywhere to be found.

Running out of places to search on the small farm, they headed toward the cattle field, feet still covered in shit-soaked shoes. Gradually a horrific howling could be heard. Unable to imagine what could be causing such a terrible din, they ran to find the source. Maybe the old man had finally pissed off the wrong person and they'd taken him out back to even the score. Thick clogs of dirt mingled with the liquid cow waste, forcing them to abandon their final futile attempts to save their shoes. Finally spotting my grandfather in the distance with the cattle, they were relieved to see that he was still alive; not killed, but killing. He was beating a bloody bull even bloodier with a steel rod. The large brown bull was tied to a post by the ring through its nose and was bellowing for dear life. My grandfather was howling unintelligibly in German, becoming more incensed with each blow.

Accustomed to such events, Bill shrugged his shoulders, casually waved to the old man, and turned back toward the house.

No doubt he intended to sneak into the fetid kitchen and refresh himself with a few free shots. He could relax for a few minutes and await the old man's return. Appalled, Gertie took off toward my grandfather in bare feet, ruining her nylons as bushes scraped against her legs. She was screaming, crying, and begging him to stop. Bill, who found nothing unusual or disturbing about his father's onslaught, caught up to her and grabbed her by the wrist, pulling her back.

"What the hell is wrong with you? What do you think you're doing?" Long accustomed to his father's temper, he was genuinely puzzled. The blows were nothing he hadn't endured himself as a boy. Bill often bragged that he could take a beating, but he could also dish it out. He was proud of the Old Man, as he had never aimed for the face; a good ass-whuppin' never hurt anyone.

To my mother's credit, she broke away from her fiancé's grip, braved the steel rod and ran up to my grandfather. He was so surprised to see my father and a crazy woman come seemingly out of nowhere that he let her grab the rod out of his hand. Swimming upstream against such violence, which must have seemed banal when she looked back on it, took an immense toll on my mother as she rarely, if ever, repeated that act of courage against my father or his family again. It would have served her well to turn away with my father when he headed back to the house. There would be no saving the bull. The reprieve she had won was only temporary – my grandfather would be back to finish the job once Bill and Gertie left and he had refueled with a few shots. Those jobs always got finished. My mother should have turned away, and in turning away, left Bill. Left them all and run, then kept running as far away as possible. Instead, she turned toward the animal and stayed.

CHAPTER THREE

1967

"Are you doing all right, honey?" Although Mimi sounded a little worried, her head didn't budge. She was all business behind the wheel, eyes on the road, hands in the ten o'clock and two o'clock positions. She'd never been in an accident and despite her concern for me, today wouldn't be the day that she ruined her record. Her car's appearance reflected her meticulous nature. The interior of the dark blue Plymouth Fury was immaculate and still smelled new although it was over six months old. I loved taking a deep breath whenever I got into the car. The smell of Mimi's car was a tangible reminder that as long as I was with her, I would be taken care of just as conscientiously.

"Yes," I answered her clearly, making sure that she could tell that I wasn't mumbling. She sometimes said that she couldn't quite hear me, reminding me, in her tactful way, to speak up. I turned my head to face her and shook my head so that she could see out of the corner of her eye that I was still giving her my full attention, despite my brief reply. I loved my grandmother and wanted her to know that I respected her. Everyone revered Mimi. She was regal and so put together, like Queen Elizabeth II. But mostly I loved Mimi because she was kind to us and there was nothing venomous hidden beneath her graciousness. Her donuts didn't explode with a limburger cheese payout. She even let us choose the radio station when we rode with her, despite the fact that she wasn't a fan of the Beatles and probably would rather have listened to anything other than Herman's Hermits singing *There's a Kind of a Hush.*

I turned back around to silently resume watching the countryside and corn fields go by through the passenger window. I was habitually taciturn, and Mimi always asked if I was OK. Although I lied to her when she inquired, I appreciated her asking in the same way that I was grateful for the stability that she and my grandfather Bumpy provided. It was as hard to believe that she had produced my mother as it was that I was Gertie's kid. It was no stretch to figure out that Aunt Kay's sense of style and grace was an extension of Mimi; the apple hadn't fallen far from the tree in Aunt Kay's case. My mother, on the other hand, was a prickly pear in the family orchard. It's probably human nature to favor people who are most like you, so my grandparents definitely gave Kay the leading edge. Still, they loved Gertie and treated her far better than she treated them – but that didn't stop them from scratching their heads about her most of the time.

Mimi and I were on our way to her house so I could stay the weekend; her house was a welcome port in the storm of my life. My grandparents let Beth and I take turns spending weekends at their house. We were old enough not to be a pain in the ass whereas the younger two were still in the whiny stage, and neither Mimi nor Bumpy could abide a whiner. She would pick one of us up on Friday nights after she got out of work at the fabric store, the rest of the family came for dinner on Sunday and we reluctantly went home after *Walt Disney* ended. While we were there, Mimi pretty much let us do what we wanted as long as we were quiet. Despite her kindness, neither Beth nor I ever breathed a word about her daughter or our life at home. We loved and respected Mimi, but we didn't trust her. It wasn't personal. Children of chaos don't trust anyone. Besides, what could she or anyone else do about our situation?

As a bonus, I could also choose the television channel all weekend, the only exception being Bumpy's addiction to Walter Cronkite on CBS News on Friday evening. Nestled in its large wooden cabinet, my grandparents' color TV was a thing of beauty. I was mesmerized by it, especially since those weekend visits were the only time that Beth or I could watch television. Despite our weekend TV addiction, we always volunteered to help our grandparents with small chores while we were there, such as cutting the lawn or doing other things around the house. Our helpfulness had a practical side: we wanted to ensure that those weekend passes continued. Time at my grandparents provided a desperately needed break, but I couldn't turn my head off. I certainly wanted to be there, but felt internal turmoil as well. Would my sisters be OK? I worried about them when I was away, especially on Saturday evenings.

Saturday evenings were special in our home. Saturday night was Gennie night. Gennie was the mistress of both of my parents, and they would have done anything for her. Anything. Gennie reigned to the exclusion of all else, including each other and their children. Saturday was payday, and Gennie was their pet name for Genesee Cream Ale. They wouldn't shop anywhere that didn't have their Gennie. From their devotion, you would have thought the drink was a 50-year-old Macleod single-malt scotch, not a cheap beer. Gennie was exceptional because it was a twofer: in addition to its elevated alcohol content, it was dirt cheap. Taste was immaterial; I can personally attest to the fact that it was some vile shit. Wild Bill always brought two cases of the stuff home with him after work, carrying the cases stacked one upon the other and perilously balancing a bag of groceries on top that threatened to obey gravity at any second. Hands full, he'd kick at the front door till my mother scrambled to get it open. Gertie wouldn't greet him at the door any other night of the week, but on Saturday, she'd get a move on to bring him inside and give him a peck on the cheek as she helped him unload. They were a team one night a week. Team Gennie.

"Did you hear that?" Beth stage-whispered.

I leaned down from the upper bunk so I could whisper back. "Are you kidding?" I answered. "They could wake the dead with that racket."

I'd been up for a while but had kept quiet. Beth was a sounder sleeper than I was so I'd hoped that she could sleep through the yelling, but I was sort of relieved that she was awake too. If I could pretend to her that I wasn't afraid, I might be able to convince myself as well.

Beth and I had learned to deal with Team Gennie's insanity together. Had Beth not been there for me, I'm sure that my mind would have snapped completely. Beth was a lot more easygoing than I was, and she was nowhere near as confrontational with our parents, having caught on early in the game that disappearing was the best way to avoid getting your ass kicked. We were not only polar opposites in temperament, but people could barely tell that we were sisters. While I favored Scout Finch, Beth more closely resembled Elizabeth Taylor in *National Velvet*. My mother designed everyone's haircuts, so Beth had wisely decided let her hair grow out. It seemed as though Beth had quickly figured our parents' puzzle out and slid past their traps, adopting an easier, softer way of dealing with them. I could have saved myself a lot of trouble by adopting her approach.

Another slam came from the kitchen. It sounded like the refrigerator had hit the wall, but I knew it wasn't the refrigerator that was jacked up.

"Who do you think will win?" Beth whispered again.

"Who cares? I just wish they'd both shut up."

"Shut the hell up," my father bellowed. Although I felt a shudder of fear pass through me, it wasn't complete terror because I knew he wasn't howling at us.

"Big man," my mother taunted. "Feel like a big man now?"

She'd hit him where it hurt. Wild Bill was around five foot six inches on a good day. He was so height challenged that he required a pillow to prop him up high enough to see over the steering wheel of the car when he drove. He was more than sensitive about it and, like most of the men in the family, had a serious Napoleon complex.

Ol' Billy Boy had changed a lot in the thirteen years that he'd been married to Gertie. His happy-go-lucky side still came out every once in great while, but for the most part, he'd morphed into the old German. Over the years, Bill had graduated from grocery boy to meat cutter; and the daily exertion of lifting sides of cow carcasses had filled him out to mirror the powerful build of his father. Another generation, another chip off the old Vlad block.

Gertie knew how my father got when he drank. Why in the hell did she have to egg him on like that? She was just begging for trouble.

It couldn't have occurred to me at the time, but perhaps on some level, like me, my mother knew that Bill the Butcher was going to take it out on someone. Maybe she thought that with enough Gennie, she could take it too.

Another thud. Then one more. "I *told* you to shut the fuck up. You're nothing but a talking cunt."

There was no further mouth from Gertie.

There'd be no cops or complaining from the neighbors. It never once occurred to us to call the police. Besides, the rotary phone was in the dining room, right next to ground zero. The Shelenskis upstairs wouldn't bat an eye. We heard Barry occasionally teaching Shelly a lesson as well; it was domestic abuse quid pro quo.

"Can you believe those two?" Beth whispered. "What's wrong with them?"

"No idea." I replied. "But I'll tell you what: there is no way that I am going to grow up to be the assholes that they are." Despite the fact that I was hardwired to protect my siblings, there was nothing I could do to protect them from my parent's Saturday night brawls. On those Saturday nights, I would get myself through them by thinking about the weekends at Mimi and Bumpy's. In my mind, I wasn't terrified on that upper bunk with mismatched sheets and screeching parents; I was snuggled next to Mimi with her arm around me, watching Walter Cronkite intone the bad news of the world. In my imagination, all was well with me, safe and warm with my grandparents.

Sunday mornings assumed their own cadence. These mornings were the basis for Beth and me developing a lifelong habit of early rising. We wanted to enjoy as much peaceful time as possible before the repulsive orchestra of addiction began its obtrusive symphony around 10:00 a.m. Gertie always got up first. Rubbing her head in an attempt to ease Gennie's backlash while hacking her lungs out, she tottered directly over to the kitchen sink and turned the spigot on. No matter where you were in the flat, you could hear her hawk a series of phlegm into the sink for about five minutes then rinse it down the drain. Effectively clearing her lungs, she grabbed her Zippo and lit the first ciggy butt of the day.

Turning the gas stove on under the silver teapot, she silently cleared the Gennie bottles off of the kitchen table. We knew better than to break the silence. While she waited for the water to boil, she lit another cigarette off of the embers of the first one. Meanwhile, Billy Boy dragged himself into the bathroom to get ready for work. He liked to pick up a few extra hours on Sundays, but he didn't have to be in until eleven. Beth and I rolled our eyes as soon as the bathroom door closed. You could almost count down to the sounds of my father vomiting his guts out: three, two, one.... The puking noise was relieved by the gagging of dry heaves that seemed as endless as a Pennsylvania winter. I asked my mother numerous times why Bill barfed every morning. She said that he was allergic to coffee, but needed it to wake up before work. It didn't occur to me until years later that he never drank any coffee before his vomiting sessions.

Just as we'd turned a deaf ear to my mother's hawking and my father's puking in the morning, we also turned a blind eye to the bruises on my mother's arms and shoulders on those Sundays. Bill the Butcher was cunning enough to never leave marks on any of our faces. Maybe he'd learned something from the old man after all.

CHAPTER FOUR

1968

I knew from as far back as I could remember that our family was different. I'd realized it long before my mother morphed into the Imp and Saturdays became fight night. I couldn't quite put my finger on it as a child, but I'd instinctively felt that we were divergent. As time went on and my parent's derangement increased, I became aware that there was an underlying dark source of the insanity. It wasn't until I was almost a teenager that I figured out the culprit's real identity and labeled the alcoholism for what it really was.

My folks kept up appearances for a long time. To the outside world, they appeared to be the downtown version of a married Andy Griffith Wild Bill had lost his wild ways while Gertie kept house with the little Opies; every Christmas card showed a perfect 50s family. But the perfection facade was just like a Wild West storefront: perfectly painted in the front, but just an empty sagebrush lot in the back. Behind the scenes, the leading cowboy and his gal never quite made it out of the saloon. It wasn't as though Gert and Bill were normal without Gennie; the Imp was stone-cold sober to the best of my knowledge (at least, I never smelled it on her when the Imp came out). And Bill's short fuse could blow up at any moment, it certainly didn't need a drink to fire it up. But early in the day, there were at least moments of calm amidst their internal storms. However, once Gennie came into the picture, it was a sure bet that all hell would break loose. It took a long time for a kid to put the pieces together; I never found the chapter on drunks in my aged encyclopedia.

As alcoholism tightened its vice grip on Gert and Bill, they abdicated their parental roles. There was no adult to fill the vacuum in family leadership, and so as the oldest, that pretty much left me in charge. It wasn't so much that I stepped up, it was more that my parents stepped back. I pictured them somehow always forgetting to come back from the cooler to take care of the kids. They didn't typically go to the bar, they were stay-at-home drinkers. So although they were physically in the house, they were light-years away emotionally. From the time I was six, I knew that there was no one at the helm of our family ship, so I found an ill-fitting sealskin and a booster seat and grabbed hold of the family wheel with my small hands. Unfortunately I had all the responsibility of the boat captain but none of the authority, so I crafted my own brand of leadership using the only examples that I had: my parents. My folks had two devices in their toolbox of life: alcohol and violence. Since drinking was out of reach for the time being, I was left with the default trait that had served my ancestors for thousands of years – brute force. I used my singular tool for all it was worth and ruled my siblings with the Teutonic iron hand that was my birthright.

Early one cold, rainy Saturday morning I was lying on my stomach on the triple carpeted living room floor, bundled in a blanket and reading the newspaper. I tried to ignore the sounds of my mother hacking and spitting, and inwardly grimaced because I knew she'd soon want something or other. I smelled the Maxwell House coffee brewing in the kitchen and my eyes stung from the inevitable cigarette smoke that wafted in from the kitchen. Like any prey, I sensed her before she approached. I feigned unawareness and pretended that I was totally unable to tear myself away from the local weather report. Elbows on the paper and head resting on the heels of hands framing my face, I finally saw her out of the corner of my eye. I felt her slippered toe nudge my rear.

"Take a run over to the Boston Store today."

Although I wouldn't recognize her situation until well into adulthood, I now know that my mother suffered from agoraphobia. She seldom ventured outside of the house, and on those rare occasions that she did, it was to visit her parents or my father's sister.

In those days, it was easier to hide her condition. We only had one car, and my father was usually away from home at one of his two jobs. My mother didn't need a car, as she had children that she could send to the grocery store and to run errands. No one ever expected Gertie to be anywhere, and she exceeded those expectations.

I felt a harder nudge from the slipper. My mother flipped a Boston Store credit card with a list and some dollar bills paper-clipped together on the newspaper page that I was reading. The bills were for those damn smokes. You'd think she'd sweeten the deal by throwing in enough for a candy bar, but it never once occurred to her to make any deal a win-win. The Boston Store was a downtown department store, a ten block distance and an hour walk away. We didn't have bicycles, and with bus fare equaling the cost of a pack of cigarettes, we wouldn't be riding via the Erie Metropolitan Transit Authority.

With the exception of the Boston Store, my parents didn't believe in credit cards. Long before Visa, MasterCard, and American Express, their sole credit card was just for these shopping ops. My mother would make a list in the form of a note to a clerk and sign it. Beth or I was then given the mission to walk downtown to the large department store. We would go from one department to the next, marking off the list as we went. When we had everything from one department that was on the list, we would check out, handing the note to the clerk so that she could see that we weren't miniature credit card bandits. One could only assume that if we weren't credit card thieves, we weren't note forging experts, either (Beth saved that expertise for the school system). We would then consult the list, trudge to the next department, and repeat the process. After the mission was accomplished, we'd traipse back home. The trip could take the better part of the afternoon, longer in bad weather, and God forbid that we got the wrong item or something didn't fit. It would be a guarantee to plod through the process the following weekend.

Rain or shine, sleet or snow, Beth and I took turns running my mother's frequent errands, which could consist of anything from going to the corner store for Belair cigarettes, doing the weekly shopping, buying Christmas gifts, or any number of other errands that involved walking out of the front door. We both hated going and would try to convince the other one to either go in our place or to at least go with us. Saying no was not an option, as my mother's retaliation was neither brief nor pretty.

My mother stepped up and nudged the list with her slipper. She said, "Trot over to the Boston Store and pick up some white shirts and handkerchiefs for your father. They're on sale. While you're there, I need some new undies and socks. I think the iron is going, too. Better get a new one and pick up a couple packs of ciggies on the way home."

I pushed the list out of the way. "It's Beth's turn. I went the last time." I kept careful score.

The slippered foot pushed forward again, sliding the list back in front of me. "Well, then go ahead and go with her. I don't know if she can carry everything by herself." My sister was eleven, two years younger than me. She shouldn't have been going downtown by herself anyway, a thought that never occurred to my mother. I certainly hadn't a clue, as I'd been running those damn errands for years by that point. Now pissed, I leapt up and kicked the newspaper all over the floor.

"Now pick it up," my mother commanded. Instead, I gave it another kick, spreading the pages further and ripping some of them in jagged edges. She grabbed the back of my neck, those narrow fingers tightened like vice grips. "Pick up that damn paper, fold it nicely and get your butt to the store like I asked you to."

Glaring at her, I pieced the paper together and folded it.

My mother returned the glare. "Wipe that look off of your face, young lady, before I wipe it off for you."

I grabbed my coat out of the front closet and bellowed to my sister, "Beth! Let's go."

No response. This wasn't my sister's first walk around the block, and she was nowhere to be found.

I bellowed again, "Beth! Now. Let's go."

Still no answer.

My mother shoved the affronting list into my jacket pocket. "Don't lose it now," she warned.

"Where's Beth?" I asked rhetorically. My mother couldn't have cared less who went, as long as someone did, and soon. She only had a few cigarettes left.

"Go ahead and go," my mother commanded. "Beth can go the next time."

I whined, "It's her turn and I'm not even supposed to go."

My mother's mood turned black in a nanosecond, a bad sign. She snapped, "Shut the hell up and get going. I said that she'll go the next time. Go ahead and take Mary Pat. She can help you." Mary had just turned eight and was small for her age. She would be as useless to me for this errand as a steak to a Buddhist. She had been playing on the dining room floor with her dolls and two imaginary friends (Trail and Trailer) during the exchange.

She brightly chirped, "I'll go! Trailer said that she'd like to go, too!"

Mary was a gentle soul who loved animals and was secretly my favorite. Even at her young age, she had a strong resemblance to Winona Ryder. I loved Beth and she was my best friend, but we were far closer in age and fought a lot like evenly matched siblings will. But Mary Pat was seven years younger than me and I was more protective toward her. She still had the fragile innocence of the young and I really wanted her to keep it as long as she could. My youngest sister had not yet been battle-hardened by my mother's never-ending stream of to-dos. Evidently, neither had Trailer. Trail had obviously wised up and was sequestered out of sight, probably sharing a hidey hole and commiserating with Beth.

Like a CEO providing strategy and confident that the executive team would provide the tactics, my mother mentally dismissed Mary, me, and the strong, silent Trailer. She untangled the long phone cord and moved the beige phone into the kitchen. Settling in at the table for a midday gabfest, she lit a cigarette with the Zippo and poured a cup of the freshly brewed coffee. Although she couldn't be convinced to walk out the front door, my mother was not antisocial. Her favorite hobby was engaging in marathon phone fests with anyone who would answer the phone. Often lasting four or five hours, the phone-a-thons terminated only when one of the participants finally had to go to the bathroom. Mrs. Shelenki upstairs was a favorite phone confidant, but a personal visit would have required changing from the daily uniform of slippers and bathrobe for both of them. The phone, ashtray, and stained coffee cup provided immediate gratification without the bother.

Happy about the unexpected opportunity to escape the house and for the chance to have an adventure with me, Mary quickly bundled up in her warmest plaid wool coat, red knit hat and black plastic rain boots. As we trudged away from the house in the rainy mist, she chattered merrily to Trailer. It was like listening in on a one-sided telephone conversation.

After a few blocks of silence on my part, I mumbled, "What homework to do you have?"

Surprised at the sudden interruption when her conversation with Trailer was going so well, Mary was dumbfounded. "What?"

Despite my intentions on trying to shield her from my parents, my rage came out of nowhere. "I didn't stutter. What goddamn homework do you have?"

Perhaps it was a whispered warning from Trailer, or maybe it was the fact that I sounded just like my parents...either way, Mary knew that the shit was headed for impact with the fan. Her chirpiness was now a memory. "I don't know." She started to cry.

Since I wanted to cry almost every day of my life and wouldn't allow myself, I had little patience for sobbing siblings. I backhanded her, my knuckles impacting hard across the back of her head and knocking her red knit hat off of her head. Her dark tangled hair was soaked almost immediately in the pouring rain. She sobbed harder, no doubt wishing she'd kept her head low in the dining room and remained happily playing with her pals and her dolls. I gave her a rough shove and she fell into the cold, soggy mud of someone's front yard. As she hit the ground, one of Beth's long-haired troll dolls fell out of her coat pocket. Beth loved those ugly things and had a large collection of them that she treasured. Mary liked to play with them when she could get away with it. At the sight of the doll I became completely unhinged, experiencing an alcoholic's rage without needing a drop of alcohol.

"What the hell?" I screamed at my terrified sister. "You can't wait to go to the goddamn store, then you have no idea what homework you have, and now you've stolen Beth's doll!" I raged, making no sense at all, even to myself. "Get the hell out of here. Go home and do your homework and put Beth's doll back before I decide to kill you."

Mary Pat tore off down the wet pavement toward home. I turned around and plodded onward toward the Boston Store. In retrospect, I wasn't angry at Beth and Mary. I didn't want my sisters to be old before their time like I was, but I didn't know how to say that. I didn't even know how to feel it. I wanted my sister to remain with her dolls and her imaginary friends on the warm dining room floor near the heater. I didn't want her to slog through the sleet for several miles dragging crap that my parents should have been handling, no matter how much of an adventure she thought that it would be.

I was livid with my parents, not with my sister. What I wanted more than anything was for Bill and Gert to act like real parents and for us to just be regular kids. But by then, it was too late for all of that...far too late.

CHAPTER FIVE

1973

Aunt Kay sat at her dining room table late one Sunday morning finishing the last swallow of coffee and working the New York Times crossword puzzle. Working that crossword was her favorite weekly treat, and like Mimi, she was good at it. It was a rare week when she couldn't complete the puzzle. High in the eastern sky, she could feel the sun toasting her back through the large dining room window. She hoped that summer wouldn't take its usual sweet time arriving. If it would warm up just a tad, she could open the windows to enjoy the May breeze coming off of Lake Erie. Jerry Vale played on the stereo and she hummed along with her favorite songs.

Just a few squares away from finishing the puzzle, a knock on the front door infringed on her concentration. Surprised by the interruption, she put the paper down to answer it. As she opened the large wooden door, she was astounded to find my mother standing there. The last time her sister had visited her home had to have been five Christmases ago. It was like seeing Marley's ghost out of season, and Marley looked like hell. My mother's eyes were bloodshot and brimming with tears. Gertie's hair looked like someone had run through it with an egg-beater, and it appeared as though she'd slept in yesterday's clothes. She had a bubble of snot coming out of her nose which she wiped away with the sleeve of her light blue jacket, punctuating her ensemble. Aunt Kay had never seen her looking so disheveled. Since the crack epidemic was still ten years away, she'd never yet seen anyone looking so scuzzy in public. She gaped at her sister, too surprised to invite her in. Aunt Kay peered past her to see where Billy Boy and the kids were, but my mother was alone. My aunt opened the screen door to let her in, but remained speechless.

"I left him," my mother announced as she pushed past her sister and flopped on the sofa. Aunt Kay stood by the door in a state of shock.

"You, you left who?" my aunt stammered.

Although my parent's battles had been escalating for years, no one else ever saw the bruises or endless piles of empty brown bottles. Their families were still in the dark about the drinking and fighting. Aunt Kay wondered if my father had a new girlfriend. My mother had confessed years ago to Aunt Kay that she had proof that Wild Bill rode again and again with many women over the years. Although Gertie's feeling were hurt, Bill's extramarital affairs didn't surprise nor particularly trouble my aunt, as she really didn't expect men to be saints once they were married. She tried unsuccessfully to convince my mother that it wasn't personal, it's just how it was. Both of her husbands had cheated on her and if she weren't so good at crossword puzzles, she probably would have defined monogamy as a fine, dark wood.

Aunt Kay had firsthand experience that Billy Boy was an asshole. He'd made a few passes at her when he'd had a few too many. One afternoon, she had been alarmed to wake from a nap at my parents' house to find his bodiless hand trying to grope her. Hiding under the bed, only his arm was visible as his hand flopped from side to side trying to cop a feel. He was busted for the fucking idiot that he was when she started screaming. Although she knew that boys will be boys and cut them a lot of slack, that had been a bad line to cross, even in her book. But aside from my father's carousing and drinking, she thought that Gertie didn't have much to complain about. Hadn't she found a husband in spite of herself? Like everyone else, Aunt Kay thought that life was good for my mother. Bill always came home eventually, my mother didn't have to work, and the bills always got paid somehow. It wasn't a life that she would have wanted, but she was glad for her sister. She'd always considered my mother a fool for marrying Wild Bill in the first place, but a relatively happy fool. It conveniently slipped her mind that she'd introduced them in the first place.

"I left that son of a bitch, that's who." My mother started to cry again.

My aunt sat down next to her on the couch and handed her a box of tissues to avoid another snot episode. Aunt Kay still struggled to wrap her head around the reality shift as her mind fired rapidly through various improbable scenarios. Her sister couldn't have left Bill; a sane person would have left him years ago. Since she'd put her time in for this long, my aunt figured it was "until death do we part". But who else could she have left, since she'd been housebound for ten years? The only other unrelated male that she regularly came in contact with was the radish man, an ancient Russian who sold tomatoes and radishes from his Western Flyer red wagon through the neighborhood in the summer.

Against her common sense, Aunt Kay threw up a test balloon. "You left Bill?"

"Of course that's who I left," my mother snapped through her tears. "Who the hell else would I leave?"

Aunt Kay asked incredulously, "Why?" There were so many reasons, she couldn't think of just one. She couldn't wait to hear the answer.

"Because he's a drunken asshole." It was though my mother had finally received her formal introduction to reality, eighteen years too late. She removed her jacket and raised the sleeve of her rumpled blouse to show the latest round of bruises.

Aunt Kay gaped. She said, "Oh, my God. I'll kill that son of a bitch. What happened?"

"All he does is drink. He won't stop, and I'm tired of being his punching bag. I've tried to get him to go to AA, but that didn't work. I just can't take it anymore." My mother's sobs escalated. She'd finally told someone the truth after all those years. "Can I stay here?" she pleaded.

My aunt knew my father. She realized that he would show up at the door sooner rather than later. She also knew his temper and strength. If he was slamming my mother around, he wouldn't hesitate to do the same to her if she took her sister in. He might even throw an extra punch or two in, since she'd busted him on his touchy-feely escapade under the bed. My mother clearly couldn't stay. Aunt Kay lit two cigarettes and handed one to her sister.

"You sit right there and calm down. I'll go make us some coffee." As she went to the kitchen, she grabbed the beige Princess phone from the dining room and took it with her out of earshot. As she waited for the coffee to percolate, she dialed the rotary phone to discuss her dilemma with her best friend Pat.

Barely giving her pal time to say hello, she said, "My sister just landed in my living room she finally left her goddamn husband and wants to hide out here Judas Priest he's a dumbass but even he is smart enough to know that she'll fly straight here like a homing pigeon if that son-of-a-bitch finds her in this house he'll light her up and me too what in the hell should I do?" It all came out in one long run-on sentence. Aunt Kay talked fast to begin with, but her mouth could move faster than a clapper on a duck's ass when she was anxious. After all, Billly Boy could show up any minute.

"Chill, Katherine." Pat was always in control in a military Zen sort of way. Her husband was an Army lifer and if she'd learned nothing else from moving around the country with the armed services, she'd at least learned how to deal with almost anything in a matter-of-fact way. She was also the only person who always called my aunt by her full name. "Gert can stay at my house."

It still never occurred to anyone to call the police or to file charges against my father for assault and battery. All three of those women would have been stunned if someone had suggested it, as would almost anyone else of that time. You handled your own problems; you surely didn't hang them out for strangers to deal with, no matter how much it may have helped.

"What did you say?" Aunt Kay was so surprised that she choked on her cigarette smoke and started coughing.

Pat lived in Northeast, a small town in grape country near the Pennsylvania border of New York, about twenty miles outside of Erie. Bill the Butcher had never met Pat, so he had no idea where she lived. Her home would be the ideal place for my mother to go underground. In the days before safe houses for abused women, my mother was offered refuge through the kindness of a practical stranger. Although Pat was Aunt Kay's best friend, Gertie's penchant for isolation meant that she'd only met her once or twice. She barely knew Pat.

"Katherine? Are you OK?" Pat asked, still listening as my aunt choked.

"I'm fine. What did you say?" she repeated. Pat's response had not been what she'd expected. She wanted to ensure that she'd heard her friend correctly.

"I said that she can stay at my place. Sammy and I can stay with my parents for a while and Gert can have the house. It will give me some time to spend with my folks anyway."

Pat and her three-year-old son had just moved back to Erie while her husband was stationed in Korea for thirteen months. Pat and her child immediately vacated their home for a couple of weeks so that my mother and siblings would be safe and Gert could figure out her next move. One would think that Gertie would be eternally grateful for Pat's kindness. After all, Pat had probably saved her from a beating so severe that it could have finally put her in the hospital or killed her. Wild Bill never got accustomed to rejection from women and didn't take it well, although he should have gotten used it as many times as it happened in the later years of his drinking. Gennie had exacted her toll on his looks, and, like many alcoholics, his once sharp and chiseled features were surrounded by alcoholic bloat. He still loved the ladies and couldn't handle the fact that they didn't love him quite as much anymore. His only criteria for hitting on someone was that she was alive, and he probably would have waived that requirement if he'd had enough to drink.

In the years to come, my mother only spoke with Pat one more time after she'd left the house in grape country. She personified the old joke: what's the difference between an alcoholic and a dog? If you rescue a dog, you'll have a loyal friend for life. If you rescue an alcoholic, they'll bite your hand off and then piss on your leg.

Gert didn't stay separated from Billy Boy at that time. I was puzzled when she went back and more than slightly disgusted with her lack of courage. When I asked her about it in later years, she simply snapped that she didn't have "the opportunity", a statement that puzzled and enraged me even more. He hadn't had a gun to her head and she wasn't a hostage, what "opportunity" was it that she required? However, after my hatred began to subside years later and after a great deal of my own personal work, I came to understand the situation from her point of view – like almost all battered women, she had no self-esteem left after years of being verbally and physically assaulted. She had barely left the house in a decade and had no financial resources, as she hadn't worked since she'd gotten married and my father controlled the household money. She was suddenly going to be independent? In retrospect, it would have been more surprising if she *had* managed to stay away. I imagine that it would be akin to someone living in complete darkness for years and then walking out into bright sunlight: a welcome experience, but blinding and overwhelming. However, although she went scrambling back into the darkness, once that door had opened for Gertie, it didn't close back quite as tightly.

That incident was the beginning of the end for them. Within a year, my parents finally, blessedly divorced; proof positive that even hell will end eventually. After a few crocodile tears, Wild Bill moved on to greener pastures and younger fillies. Gertie got to keep the house. They both got what they really wanted.

As my parents were preoccupied with their squabbles, I seized the opportunity and moved out. I gambled that each one would think that I was with the other, and the gamble paid off. I knew that neither of them would miss me, but they would miss the maid service that I provided. Alcoholics aren't particularly interested in maintaining themselves or their surroundings, but they are quite keen on someone else doing it for them. When I left, Cinderella's frock was passed to Beth, who wore it for a short while and then moved out as soon as she could. Mary saw the writing on the wall and immediately called her boyfriend to come and get her. She wasn't yet a high school junior when she fled from my mother and moved in with her boyfriend and his parents.

Although I could finally escape, I had nowhere to go and no cash to get there. It was like blasting off into space with no destination and no fuel: you're rapidly going to wind up right back where you started, a lot worse for wear. I'd graduated from high school, but I had no job and no car. I traveled everywhere by bus or by friend. Aunt Kay again came to the rescue. She got me a job where she worked and her friend Sharon allowed me to sleep on her couch. Aunt Kay, Sharon, and I carpooled so I had least had a roof over my head, a job, and a way to get back and forth between the two.

Sharon lived in a tiny apartment over a barber shop that had once been an attic. Her tiny place was barely big enough to hold Sharon's things, let alone a roommate. Although I only had a couple of suitcases, it would still be a tight fit – but she took a deep breath and we both squeezed in. She had a busy dating life and also worked a second job, so for the first time in my life, I had a lot of quiet time alone. I found the apartment far too silent after the chaos of my parents' house. It was an odd feeling after spending almost my entire life dodging one drunken crisis after the other. I had no idea what to do with myself when I wasn't working. After a couple of months, my feelings started to thaw just a tad. I had no point of reference for feelings and did not care one little bit for the ones that I felt when they started.

You would think that I would have been relieved and ecstatic to finally escape the little house of alcoholic horrors. I thought so too. I anticipated living happily ever after since it wouldn't matter what happened to me; anything would be better than where I'd come from. This wasn't my first vacation away from the House of Crazy. I'd run away from home many times, but could never manage to stay away for long because I felt guilty for leaving my siblings. What if Gertie had an Imp episode while I was on vacation? Still, I sometimes had to leave to cool off. I'd often thought seriously about killing one of my parents after some episode or other, but I knew that I couldn't afford a good lawyer. I once walked fifteen miles to the house of a family friend to decompress after my mother abused a dog and I thought that I would finally go over the edge and take her out. But after I'd been away for a day or so, I'd inevitably worry about our dog or my siblings and return home. My parents usually welcomed me back with a beating and then ignored me for a few days until they needed something.

Instead of finally feeling free at Sharon's, I was one big bundle of nerves. I had the anxiety of a cat on an electrified roof. If I thought that I'd felt guilty before about leaving Beth and Mary Pat, it was now magnified a hundred times. Who would protect them now that I couldn't any longer? Every feeling was a startling, painful jolt and I couldn't space them out any more. I'd been living with the stress of alcoholic drama for so long, it was almost as though I was lost when it was missing. Drama creates a high, like walking a high wire without a net and not knowing if you'll survive. That high can turn children of alcoholic parents into drama junkies, which is exactly what I'd become. I didn't know any other way of life. It occurred to me at the time that I thought I knew how combat veterans felt when they returned home from war: that there is nothing left to fight any more. There's no jolt, there's no juice. Now what? I decided that I needed to die, and became obsessed with suicide.

While living in the combat zone of my parent's house, I was too consumed with anticipating their next move and plotting potential counter-moves to have any feelings whatsoever. I often plotted their demise, never my own. It wasn't until I was away from them that I started to think about killing myself. I would make several weak attempts over the next couple of years, mostly with valium. I didn't have a gun and was too chicken to hang myself. I wanted to die, but I didn't want it to be painful; I was in enough emotional pain as it was. However, I always woke up afterward. I never knew how many to take and there wasn't a handy search engine to consult at the time.

I began to draw on my arms with razor blades, but lacked the courage to really put a couple of deep lines across my wrists and finish the job. The razors became my solution for anxiety. When I felt squirrely, which was often, I'd break out the razors. I was astounded when I started hearing of teens cutting themselves within the last several years, since I thought that I had invented that habit and I'd never told anyone about it. It was another one of my little secrets. As soon as Sharon would leave the apartment, I'd break out the razors. Somehow I felt better when I was bleeding. The cuts weren't deep, and I never permanently injured myself. But what I lacked in depth of cutting, I made up for in quantity. The cuts were all over my upper arms and forearms. I hoped that the cuts would get infected and I would die. No one had a clue, as I always wore long sleeves. Since everyone in Pennsylvania wears long sleeves, it wasn't difficult to hide the marks. I also took to putting cigarettes out on my arms, which didn't heal as quickly. But since the burns lasted longer, I eventually stopped burning. With the pretzel logic that I had at the time, I thought they would be harder to explain if someone saw them. Of course, since I tended to cut myself in geometric patterns, the cuts wouldn't have been any picnic to explain, either. But clear thinking wasn't high on my list of skills at that time.

My default decision-making criterion growing up was to figure out what my parents would do in any given situation and do the exact opposite. It's a rather narrow criterion, quite prone to error, and it didn't fit every situation by far. But it was the only tool in my shed at the time, and if you're going to build a house, having a screwdriver is at least a start. As I grew up, I affirmed at least a couple million times, "I am never going to be like them."

Since I believed that my parents' only problem was drinking, my Prime Directive was easy: Don't Drink. It wasn't as though it was a sacrifice. I didn't like the taste of liquor and had gotten sick the few times I drank as a teen. From my perspective, I was clearly not cut out to be a drinker. Not only that, I was made of sterner stuff than my parents. They were weak and didn't have my willpower. I felt more than a slightly superior, a German trait that put me closer to being cut from the same cloth than not. Fortunately, I had no idea at the time that I wasn't as far from being like them as I liked to think that I was.

I finally started to make some friends who dabbled in drugs. Drugs were acceptable to me because they didn't violate my Prime Directive. I wasn't drinking, so it was all OK. Drugs provided a way for me to make friends, but still left me able to comfortably fit into my overcoat of superiority over my alcoholic family.

I found the effects of marijuana disappointing. For all of the hype, I'd hoped for much more. I remember keeping a journal at the time and once wrote that the only thing that pot did for me was change my personality. Although I wasn't unhappy that my personality changed, as I wasn't particularly fond of it to begin with, I really wanted to change how I felt. Although pot was an interesting buzz, it didn't get me anywhere near where I wanted to go. Weed was a good step, but it was like expecting to go on vacation to Disneyland and winding up playing putt-putt.

So I branched out; I took whatever anyone had available. I didn't even ask what I was taking, as I didn't care. I'd take anything as long as it somehow changed how I felt. I still didn't have a lot of cash, and neither did my friends, so we'd score some acid or speed when we had the funds. Once we experimented with No-Doze and Pepsi because someone swore the combination created a buzz. Unfortunately for me at the time, I found that it didn't do a damn thing except keep me awake for a long time. Although I wasn't particularly impressed with the effects of drugs, I noticed that when I took them, my cutting decreased.

After a while, when anxiety struck, I'd fire up a joint instead of opening a razor. Maybe the drugs didn't take me where I wanted to go, but they at least got me away from where I shouldn't have been. I wouldn't advocate pot as a solution for current-day cutters or would-be suicides. I'm not advocating any solution, as I really have no idea where the problem stems from. I'm not a mental health professional, nor do I have any official psychological or pharmaceutical training. I was just in so much internal pain at the time that I couldn't bear it. Cutting externalized the pain and changed the way that I felt. I didn't feel better, just different. But the pain was enough to get me by that I felt a little less like killing myself, just for that moment. When I smoked pot instead, I substituted one method of changing my feelings for another. That's all I could really hope for at the time – to feel differently. I had zero hope that I would ever feel better. That was expecting far too much. I had the same singular accomplishment daily: I made it to bed alive.

CHAPTER SIX

1974

Before my parents divorced, my mother insisted that we eat supper as a family every night; she wanted it to be a bonding experience. It was a beautiful sentiment that had absolutely no chance of success. Rival prison gangs have a better opportunity for connecting over a meal than we did. Prisoners at least scream at each other, which is some form of conversation. Dinners in our home were inevitably a long, silent affair. We ate in complete silence, the abyss between us rarely traversed with communication. It is difficult, if not impossible, to build relationships in a vacuum. We kids rarely spoke unless we were spoken to, and my parents hadn't had a thing to say to each other for years that didn't involve fisticuffs. That time of day was also a six-pack away from my father's sweet spot and any conversation opened the possibility of lighting the short fuse to his temper. It would take at least another six or seven Gennies to take the edge off of life for him. In the meantime, he told us that silence is golden; shut up and get rich.

One summer evening just before my junior year in high school, we were eating at the usual muted supper table when I decided to break the silence and say what was on my mind. I'd been thinking about something important and wanted to ensure that I had my parents' full attention.

"I'm going to college, and then to the university," I announced.

Part of me knew better than to bring this subject up during "family time". But another part of me wanted my parents' undivided attention and hopefully, support. It was like I was bringing a proposal to a hostile board to secure their financial commitment for a pet project. But I had no concept of that at the time. I did know that I was playing with fire, provoking my father at a rare time when he wasn't already pissed off. It was like I was doing an impression of a kamikaze pilot. I had my answer immediately.

"Shut the hell up," my father barked without glancing up from his pork chops and mashed potatoes. As usual, he was still dressed in his work clothes, but he'd loosened his tie so he could relax at dinner. There was dried blood splattered on the sleeves and shoulders of his short-sleeved white shirt. You could almost see a bloody outline where his butcher's apron hadn't quite covered the shirt. In the silence, I could hear his dentures click as he ate. His massive paws never quit shoveling food into his mouth, an indication that although he was irritated, he wasn't seriously pissed. Fortunately, his dinner plate remained on the table instead of decorating the wall. "Girls don't go to college. That's the stupidest damn thing I've ever heard. Now shut the hell up or I'll warm your goddamn keister."

I knew that I'd pushed the topic far enough for the time being, so I zipped it to ensure that I escaped my father's wrath unscathed. However, just because I didn't talk about college anymore didn't mean that I quit thinking about it. The prospect was very unusual for someone in our family, and I knew it. What I didn't understand at the time was why I even considered it. It wasn't as though I had a specific career aspiration. Although I had a vague idea what a major was, I had no interest in any specific field of study. It was like I had inexplicably morphed into an education zombie, somehow programmed to lurch toward some phantom college in the future that I couldn't visualize but only vaguely sensed somewhere beyond everyday life.

Although I didn't comprehend it then, I later realized that continuing my education would further separate me from the life that my parents led. Neither of them had any intellectual curiosity or any concern whatsoever for anything that didn't affect them personally. They had no interest in current events, sports, or hobbies. From my perspective, if ignorance was bliss, then they were ecstatic. College would be one more rung in the ladder that I was building to escape from their homemade hell. I couldn't have articulated it then, but as I grew up I came to observe that adults primarily have two choices in making a living: they can work with their hands, or their heads. There are a few professions that use both, but it usually comes down to one or the other. I knew that schooling would be costly, but as the columnist Ann Landers once noted: "If you think education is expensive, try ignorance."

But once I moved out of the house, I was far too busy cutting, scoring nickel bags, and fixating on suicide to leave much time for plotting out an education strategy. Then, one hot Saturday afternoon, as I sweltered in the tiny apartment and gazed out of an open window through the cannabis haze, it hit me.

Lounging on Sharon's second-hand couch, I was test driving my new headphones; Pink Floyd's Dark Side of the Moon were testing the limits of my eardrums. I had the stereo turned up full blast and Richard Wright loudly sang: "Kicking around on a piece of ground in your home town. Waiting for someone or something to show you the way."

"Bullshit," I thought lazily through my buzz. I make my own way. Followers are losers. No one had ever shown me a damn thing, and I wasn't waiting on anyone to start at this stage of the game.

Soaked in sweat, I coaxed the last hit out of the joint that I held with surgical hemostats and leaned over to exhale out of the open window. I fanned myself with one of Sharon's old People magazines, hoping for just a hint of a breeze. She had a fan in her boudoir, but it did little to move any of the humid air outside of that tiny room. I hoped that she was on a date and would be out for a while. Even though the window was open, she'd be able to smell the pot. Sharon wasn't a stoner, and wasn't particularly appreciative when I fired up. Not only was it illegal, it was also a reminder that I was spending money on something else besides rent, and that my share would probably be late again.

Pink Floyd and Acapulco Gold continued their comfortable journey together inside my head. I pushed Sharon and the rent out of my conscience so I wouldn't bring myself down. Pleasantly buzzed, I idly looked out the window, watching traffic as the music continued.

"And then one day you find ten years have got behind you. No one told you when to run, you missed the starting gun."

I wondered where I'd be in ten years. It had never occurred to me before. Then, like a lightning bolt interrupting the hot summer sky, the clearest thought that I'd had in months ripped through my stoned musings. "I sure as shit missed the starting gun. What about college?" I jumped up so suddenly that I almost knocked over the paint can that was supporting the middle of the couch. My buzz was pretty much trashed. "Fuck me. Now what?" I said to myself. I could barely afford rent, let alone tuition.

My parents had made it clear that it would be laughable to look to either of them for any kind of support. I had no idea that there were student loans or grants available; I thought that everyone paid their own way. That was obviously out of the question in my case. Even more ludicrous, I had no "career goals", as my guidance counselor had called them in high school. Some of my classmates had early designs on some type of profession like teaching or medical school. But for me, the concept of a long-term career was as remote as suddenly speaking a foreign language or beaming up to an alien craft. Everyone in my social circle had somehow fallen into their job. Aside from my father, most adults I knew either worked in a local manufacturing plant or were married to someone who was (neither of which held any interest for me). I knew that I basically had zero resources and a roadmap with no marked routes.

A few weeks later, I rode my bike over to my mother's house to see Beth. Since I was no longer forced to speak to my parents, I did so only when it was unavoidable. Seeing my siblings was one of the few reasons that could induce me to visit my parents' house. As I got closer to the house, I was relieved to see Beth sitting on a neighbor's porch down the street. I took a deep breath of relief; I was off the hook for an encounter with my mother. Swinging on the porch swing with some of her friends, Beth and her pals were playing their favorite game: trolling for cute guys. Beth and her friends weren't sluts; the fun was in the game. Sometimes they'd score dates, but it didn't seem to matter. It was just the sport of it all. It was their number one summer activity and they spent hours in preparation, putting on makeup and picking out just the right outfit. It was a hobby that mystified me. I'd hang out with them for a while, but never understood their attraction to this particular sport. When I stopped to think about it, I was puzzled why I never found the trolling game as much fun as they did. A few years later, I would come to understand that my gay memo just hadn't arrived yet.

As I rolled my bike up to the porch, I waved to the Revlon gang. "Hey, any hits tonight?" It was a rhetorical question. If there had been any testosterone within miles, they would have sensed it and called it in like a giant tractor beam. And if there had been any dudes already with them, they wouldn't have seen me if I'd driven by in a parade. I parked the bike out of sight. I didn't want to decrease their chances if the luck gods smiled on them and sent a carful of cuteness their way. I joined them on the stoop. "What's going on?"

Expecting the usual shoulder shrug, I was greeted instead with a big announcement. One of the blonde Mueller twins smirked and said, "Guess who joined the army today."

"Who in the hell would do that?" I asked. The Vietnam War and the draft had ended the year before. Everyone I knew was a peace-loving protestor against the war. We were violent inside the home; we wanted peace outside of it. Aunt Kay even knew some nuns who had protested by chaining themselves to the White House fence and gotten themselves thrown in jail for their trouble.

"Me." The Mueller twin's smirk grew wider.

She could have said that she'd been abducted to the recruiting station by an alien dressed in fatigues and I couldn't have been any more surprised. Women in the Army? What the hell? I didn't know that women had been allowed in the Army since WWII ended and the Women's Army Corp and Rosie the Riveter were sent home. Besides, who would want to join?

"Why would you do that?" She'd never struck me as crazy before.

"I want to get out of this two-horse town and travel the world. Besides, I might meet a rich officer." She added, "And I can go to college on the G.I. Bill."

I'd heard of the program; it was a government deal that enabled veterans to go to college on Uncle Sam's dime. "What? Are you sure?" I asked. "I think that's just for the guys who went to Vietnam."

She shook her head. "No, the recruiter specifically said that any active service member can use it. You don't have to be a Vietnam vet."

"Really?"

"Really." Her smirk grew wider.

I smiled back this time. Bingo. There it was; my road to the Promised Land. If I had believed in God, I would have silently sent up a prayer of gratitude.

Beth jumped up off of the rocking porch lounger she'd been sitting in and said, "I gotta go. You know how she is about curfew."

Erie's summer days are just as bright and long as the winter days are brief, dark, and gloomy. Since it was almost dark, we knew that her 9:30 curfew was close. Although Beth was seventeen that summer, my mother's curfew decrees were not to be taken lightly. My sister took off down the street. I stayed a few minutes longer and quizzed the Army's newest recruit about army logistics and then retrieved my battered blue Schwinn. I'd have to haul ass, as I was a half hour bike ride from Sharon's and had to work the next day.

Riding past my mother's house, I saw my grandfather's green Dodge D100 pickup truck parked across the street. Although Bumpy was a frequent summer visitor, dropping off bushels of produce that he'd harvested, he was usually long gone by nightfall. Seeing him would be worth having to deal with my mother. I wheeled around and swung into Gertie's driveway. Pushing the bike down the drive, I heard loud shrieks and howling coming through the window. What the hell? I was still cautious around my mother and would have ordinarily taken off at the first sound of trouble, or at least listened outside the window until I'd figured out what was going on. But one of the screams sounded like Beth.

I threw the bike onto the overgrown lawn and cleared the back stoop. Flinging the screen door open, I stormed into the back porch and stopped dead in my tracks at the kitchen doorway. Bumpy stood in the middle of the kitchen, his face twisted with rage. Although he was facing me, he didn't seem to register that I was there. He wore a ratty old undershirt, grey work pants, and ankle boots: his farming clothes. His rock-hard muscles were visible under the t-shirt. Although he was in his early sixties, his hair hadn't yet begun to grey and it wasn't hard to imagine the Olympic-hopeful wrestler that he'd once been. Beth's long, dark hair was wrapped around his gnarled fist, which he used to fling her against the kitchen sink. When he let go, she fell to the floor in a heap.

Dressed in her favorite pink print summer pajamas, my mother hopped up and down in the doorway that separated the kitchen and dining room screaming with delight. I was reminded of the Imp's resemblance to a maniacal Chuckie years ago. "That's it! Show her!" she howled demonically. Her brown eyes shone brightly and a broad smile lit up her face. "Show her that she can't come home when she damn well feels like it. You come home on TIME!" She fairly danced with glee. Beth remained on the floor, racked with sobs. Her long dark hair covered her face.

In shock, my feet were glued to the floor of the back porch as though it were coated with flypaper. I couldn't have gone any further into that room if you had put a gun to my head. Accustomed though I was to my father's beatings, I'd never seen anything like this from my mother's father. How could this be my Bumpy? What the hell had happened to him? Had he always been like that and we never knew? Or had he suddenly been possessed by the same demons that seemed to inhabit my parents?

Too confused and frightened to say a single word, I stood there in shock. Violence from my parents didn't bother me. I pretty much expected it from them, they were hard-wired for it. But not my grandfather, it couldn't be. It was though the earth had suddenly turned upside down and begun revolving backwards. Frozen and mute, I must have seemed invisible. Beth's scarlet face was twisted with grief.

Bumpy got down on his hands and knees to roar in Beth's face, "You will obey your mother. Do you hear me? Obey! If she tells you to be home by 9:30, it does not mean whenever you feel like waltzing in. If this happens again, you'll have me to deal with." To emphasize his threat, he roughly seized another handful of hair and yanked Beth back up from the floor. Then he gave her another toss as though practicing a gold-medal discus throw. She connected with the kitchen table and dropped again. This time she was still.

Stunned and scared shitless, I turned and tore out the back door and escaped into the night. If I were the crying kind, I would have sobbed all the way to Sharon's. But I hadn't cried in years. Tough don't cry. But I didn't feel so tough any more. I was a big sister that fell down on the job when the stakes were the highest. I'd abandoned my sister when she needed me the most. I'd not only let her down, more importantly, I'd let myself down and I had *never* done that before. But the worst thing was the feeling that I'd sunk to my father's level when he'd turned away from his father and the bull. I was ashamed of myself for my weakness. It turned out that my mother had more courage than I did, standing up to the Old German all those years ago. When it was my turn to stand up, I stood down instead. I was weak, not strong. Maybe deep down, I really was like them. It was a prospect that I couldn't bear. I had to get away, far away. If I stayed in that town any longer, I might turn out to be just like the people that I hated the most. The next day, I blew off work and joined the Mueller twin in the Army.

CHAPTER SEVEN

1974

The next morning, I gave a couple of fake coughs and asked Sharon to tell my boss that I was sick. I peeked out of the front window until I saw her drive away and immediately got dressed. I didn't know how long the recruiting process would take and wanted to complete it that day. I caught the next bus downtown and took the recruiter by surprise when he saw me waiting for him as he arrived to unlock the door. Perhaps it was the first time since the Japanese had bombed Pearl Harbor that someone couldn't wait for a recruiting station to open. After the Vietnam War and the draft ended, it wouldn't have been surprising if recruiters had been reduced to dragging in bums off the street and signing them up before they went into DTs. But there I was, at the head of a non-existent line when the door opened. It didn't occur to me to investigate any of the other branches of the military. There was no need to look around when I knew the Army had the goods I wanted.

The recruiter first assured me that women weren't sent into battle, even if Vietnam should flare up again. Despite the fact that I was against the war, I wouldn't have cared. I was on my own mission: college or bust.

Before he really launched into his pitch, I wanted to ensure that Chris, the Mueller twin, hadn't been lying. "Can I still get the G.I. Bill even though I wasn't in Vietnam?"

Sensing that he would have one less bum to drag in to make quota that month, he gave me a big smile. "You bet! Plus, we'll pay for college classes while on you're on active duty. You can save the G.I. Bill for when you get out."

Slam dunk, nothing but net. The deal was done, and we both knew it. I gave him a big grin in return.

I took the aptitude test and was informed that I had scored an IQ of 130. I had no idea what that meant, so I asked how that translated to my options. Seeing his ~~prey~~ quota getting closer, the recruiter brought out a big catalog and assured me that I could go to any school that the Army offered. My new best friend informed me in a conspiratorial tone that Uncle Sam offered a lot more career options than most people knew of.

"I'd like to learn something that I could do after I get out," I said thoughtfully, as though it were the first time that I'd considered such a thing. "Maybe psychology, or telephone pole maintenance, or TV repair." I wanted to ensure I covered a broad range of careers. "I'd also like to go someplace warmer." There were so many options that it was hard to decide. Paging through the catalog, I finally came to a decision. "That's it. I'll be a psychologist." Maybe I could figure myself out first, and then make some money figuring out my crazy family.

My new best friend looked crestfallen. As his smile faded he said, "Oh, no. I'm sorry, that school is filled for the next year."

I was stunned. Who knew that there was a whole year's worth of people with crazy families trying to figure them out?

Checking his special (quota) sheet, he broke into a conspiratorial grin. "How would you like to go to Pershing Missile Repair School? You can fix computers!"

I wasn't quite sure what a computer was, but I liked the idea of fixing something, even if it wasn't me.

A good salesman knows the right buttons to push to get to the customer to buy, and my new best friend hit them all at the same time, hard. "The school is a yearlong, and it's in Alabama." Quota sealed.

In true family tradition, I was sneaky; not breathing a word about my plans to anyone. After I'd passed the physical and was sworn in a couple of weeks later, I finally broke the news. The response was unanimous, and was one that I would have had to anyone else: "Are you nuts?" But I had my internal marching orders and went off to basic training.

For me basic turned out to be more adventure than ordeal. There was marching and drilling and yelling aplenty. But for the first time in my life, I was part of a team: something that was hardly worthy of notice for most people, but it was a really big thing for a social misfit from a crazy family. I had new friends, got to shoot big guns, and got paid for it; not a bad deal in my book. Thanks to my mother's sewing, I was accustomed to ill-fitting clothes. And thanks to her homemade haircuts, I wasn't troubled as much as some by the weeks of bad hair days caused by the required OD green cap. In many ways, my whole life had been a prelude for the Army. Screaming drill sergeants and barracks life wasn't even that bad in comparison to growing up in an alcoholic household. No Private Benjamin here; I actually felt quite at home.

The Army considered drinking during basic training a luxury to be earned. It wasn't permitted until the last couple of weekends, and there was great consternation among the troops during the dry spell. Well, almost all of the troops. I pretended to be as upset as every other recruit, but I was secretly relieved. There would be no pressure to join in extended drink fests. At that time, I still thought people who drank were soft, flaccid. I still considered alcohol to be my parent's greatest weakness, the top of a long list of their character flaws. I was still young enough to be flying high on my own sense of self-importance. At that time, I still felt that it was quite unfortunate for Bill and Gert that they hadn't been blessed like me with my strength of character, my willpower, my intelligence, and my ambition. Perhaps my arrogance would have been tempered if I could have borrowed a crystal ball and gotten a glimpse into my own future.

Although new recruits weren't allowed to do much on the weekends, attendance at Sunday church services was permitted and even encouraged. If you're going to kill a commie for Christ, you may want to send up a prayer for a good, clean shot. No needless suffering. Many of us became overnight converts, weekly attending whatever church was located across the street from the barracks. I have no idea what denomination it was because our religious zeal was directed toward a different God. While some were no doubt praying for their husbands and sons still in the jungles of Southeast Asia, my friends and I were there to escape the barracks and present burnt offerings of another sort in the parking lot. Praise the Lord and fire up the joints. The pot was scored from the burnt-out Vietnam veteran who dealt out of his scarred yellow T-Bird convertible parked near the church. The MPs had to have known he was there because he showed up week after week. Maybe they felt sorry for him. More likely, he paid them off. Either way, he was there like clockwork. Thank you, Baby Jesus. Support our vets.

After basic, I was shipped to Redstone Arsenal, Alabama for Advanced Individual Training. I'd signed up to learn how to repair the computers that guided Pershing nuclear missiles. Pershings were surface-to-surface medium-range nuclear missiles that the U.S. kept in Germany pointed toward Russia during the Cold War, deployed as part of NATO's defense to counter Russia's mobile SS20-Saber nuclear missiles. The Army maintained these missiles that moved around the German countryside on trailers. More mobile than their intercontinental long-range brothers buried in the mountains of the Rockies by the Air Force, Pershings could be kept on the move and were only a short two-hour flight to Moscow.

At Redstone, I discovered reliability – in more ways than one. Consistency and predictability were traits I hadn't even had a nodding acquaintanceship with until that point. In alcoholic families, the only thing you can count on is that you can't count on anything. An alcoholic judges themselves on good intentions, while the rest of the world judges us by our actions. Our family had gotten to the point where even intentions had long ago ceased to be a pretense.

Although introduced to computers through a quirk of Army fate, I became infatuated with their digital intelligence from the start. It was a blind date that immediately bloomed into true love. If I could have met a computer, it would have had me at hello. By their very nature, computers are dependable and undramatic. They're so logical that they make accounting look sweaty and sexy. The essence of a computer is a bit; it's either on or off. It can't be otherwise. There are no shades of grey, no half-truths, no bullshit, and no misinterpretation. On or off. Yes or no. It was the first thing I ever encountered that even alcoholism couldn't fuck up.

On a more personal level, I found consistency with a family, an unexpected encounter with normality that would alter me profoundly, although I wouldn't realize its full impact until years later. Right before I graduated from basic training, I received a letter from Aunt Kay's friend Pat (the same Pat that had given her house up for my mother). Pat's husband Sam was back from Korea and they were already stationed at Redstone. Their family was driving to Pennsylvania to visit family for Christmas (only a few weeks away), and I was told I was welcome to ride along. Although I'd met Pat and Sam a couple of times over the years, and they'd gone quite out of their way to do some really nice things for my family, I didn't know them well. Still extremely lacking in social skills, it would be a stretch for me to spend fourteen hours with people that I barely knew. I was also pretty sure that they wouldn't let me smoke pot in the back seat with their five-year-old son. However, my private's salary didn't go far, and the ride was free. I also didn't want to be a big loser and spend Christmas in the barracks. I was in for the ride, and for more than I knew.

The first weekend after arriving at Redstone, I called Pat from the pay phone in the barracks to arrange for the ride. She immediately invited me over to their quarters on base for dinner that night. I wasn't wild about the idea, as I felt as though she felt sorry for her friend's niece. But I really had nothing else to do, and besides, everyone else in the barracks was drinking. Most importantly, I was keenly aware that if I didn't go, my aunt would be on the phone the next day making me wish that I had. Aunt Kay could tell you to go to hell and make you enjoy the trip, but was just adept at ensuring that you didn't. That Irish tongue sliced both ways.

Pat arrived to pick me up a short while later in their blue and white Buick LeSabre. It was one of the nicest cars I'd ever seen. With the exception of my grandmother, most of the people I knew had cars that were held together with Bondo and duct tape. Pennsylvania winters can take a big bite out of cars as well as people.

"Hiya, momma! How you be? Who fucked up your hair?" Pat greeted me with a big grin as I got into the white leather passenger seat. She bore a faint resemblance to Bea Arthur. She was as well-put-together as Ms. Arthur, and wore a sweatshirt that read: Jesus Saves but Moses Invests. I'd only been around her for short periods of time up until that point and never quite knew what to make of her. This time was no exception.

"Hi." I gave my best impression of a smile. I had just used up 50% of my conversational arsenal for people I didn't know well.

"How's the Army treatin' ya, momma?"

"It's OK."

"Have you spoken with your awnt since you got here?"

"No. I'll probably call her later."

"We'll call her when we get to the house. I'll show you around the base first." Pat spoke in declarative sentences. Her statements fell just short of being commands; there were never any wishy-washy "maybes" or "we'll sees". Like my aunt, Pat had never been introduced to wishy-washy. Unlike my aunt, she would have given it the finger at the introduction. She drove me around the base, pointing out Redstone landmarks and firing off questions and facts so fast that I became engaged in conversation and interested in the sights in spite of myself.

"How were the drill sergeants? Did the food suck? Do you feel funny wearing those uniforms? Doesn't that rocket look like a phallic symbol? How bad did your feet hurt? The drinking age in Alabama is eighteen. Do you want to stop at the Rod and Rake? They sell beer on Sunday. What kind of beer do you want?"

"I don't drink beer." I finally got more than a word in, a personal best.

Pat shrugged. "OK. Wine? Red? White? Anything else?"

Thank God she'd dropped the momma bit. "No, thanks."

Another shrug. "OK, let's go see if the roast is ready yet."

When we arrived at their apartment, Sam was in the same location where I would see him for the next thirty-five years: sitting in front of the TV with a game on, reading. He immediately put his book down and got up when we walked in. Tall and thin with dark-rimmed glasses, Sam bore a strong resemblance to Henry Mitchell, father of Dennis the Menace. I knew from experience that Sam was a nice guy. He'd spent a summer afternoon teaching me to drive a stick shift in their Volvo P1800S at my grandmother's when I was sixteen. Despite a massive hangover, he bore my grinding through the gears of his beloved sports car without a single expletive.

"Hi, Lor!" he said as he came over and gave me a big hug. I didn't know any men that hugged.

"Hi, dear. The roast is almost ready," he greeted Pat. I also didn't know any men that called their wife "dear".

The two bedroom apartment was small enough to be cozy, but not enough to be cramped. The black leather living room sofa and chair looked comfortable and the Sunday Huntsville Times was strewn next to Sam's chair, a lifelong trait. A small Christmas tree stood in the corner with twinkling lights and some wrapped gifts were stacked neatly underneath. Art deco paintings hung on the walls and a large poster dominated the hallway near the bathroom. The poster featured a well-heeled gentleman with a champagne flute entitled *Poverty Sucks*. The dining room was separate from the kitchen and held a casual dining room set.

The pot roast did smell good, and the heat from the oven steamed the windows against the damp, chilly December afternoon. I'd only eaten mess hall fare for the past ten weeks and although I had gained ten pounds during basic training, it wasn't due to overeating. An Army runs on its stomach and feet, and Army cooks take no chances that your feet will fail from the lack of calories in your stomach.

"Relax, sit down! Can I get you a drink?" Sam refilled his own bourbon and water. He seemed awfully chipper but didn't appear sloshed.

"Um, no thanks."

A slightly chubby little towhead with large brown eyes wandered out from his room, a miniaturized version of Mr. Mitchell's Dennis. Sam introduced me to their son, Sammy, as the kid and I took each other's measure. He didn't smile. I wondered if he was a whiner like most only children.

"Hi. Do you want to play a game with me?"

No whine. So far, so good. "OK." I agreed, rewarding the kid for the whine-free zone.

Sammy and I sat on the living room floor and played Chutes and Ladders while I chatted with Sam about the Army. Within a short while, Pat announced that dinner was ready. Over dinner, we chatted about family, the upcoming drive, and some more Army talk. But they also wanted to discuss politics and current events, which surprised me. I didn't know anyone who had the least interest in anything besides the basics of life: drinking, drugging, and getting paid or getting laid.

After dinner, Pat called my aunt. Although I'd gotten some letters from her, I hadn't spoken with her since I left home. As we passed the phone back and forth like a volleyball, I found myself laughing and joking. Sam occasionally joined in the conversation from the living room. After we hung up, Pat drove me back to the barracks and ended the most normal afternoon of my nineteen years.

CHAPTER EIGHT

1975

I spent a lot of time with Pat and Sam during and after the road trip – in fact, I spent most weekends with them. They had a boat and taught me to water ski. They didn't mind if I brought a book to Sammy's soccer games as long as I put it down to cheer in the appropriate places. Pat took me to her hairdresser and I got a decent hairstyle for the first time in my life. Their friends thought that they had basically adopted me. Pat would tell them that I was Sam's daughter from a previous marriage; and when the friends would comment that they didn't know that Sam had been married before, we'd exclaim, "He wasn't!" The friends would scratch their heads and we would giggle.

In a storybook world, Pat, Sam, and Sammy would have been the kindly family that I never had. Sam and Pat would have been Auntie Em and Uncle Henry to my Dorothy, or June and Ward Cleaver with Sammy as the Beaver. They would have taken me to church and Pat would have taught me knitting. But they weren't storybook people, and I wouldn't have had any use for them if they had been. Alcoholic families aren't particularly nice, and although my family's violence terrified me, I still didn't particularly care for nicey-nice people. I found them dull and boring. There's a certain edge that goes with the unpredictability of an alcoholic home, and it can be as addicting as the booze. Human beings seem to be hard-wired to love surprise and drama, and alcoholic families provide that in spades. Like an animal that develops a lust for blood, once you have an appetite for alcoholic theatrics, it doesn't abate. Spending too much time around nice people was akin to watching paint dry.

Fortunately, despite the fact that my faux adopted family wasn't alcoholic, they could be sarcastic and somewhat snarky so I felt right at home in that regard. Sam was a talker. An instructor and part-time radio announcer, he had a deep, resonant speaking voice. He was extremely well-read and could hold forth on any topic for hours, which I loved and Pat tolerated. After nineteen years of living with basic illiterates, I was starved for intellectual conversation and Sam delivered. He loved a good audience, and I loved to hear his deep voice talk about politics, history, and any other bullshit that he thought up. But Pat had been subjected to his lectures for years and the blush was off of that rose.

When she'd had enough, she'd take a deep drag from her Benson and Hedges and exhale in a commanding voice that would have made a First Sergeant proud, "Sam, shut the fuck up and let someone else talk for a change."

I'd freeze and wait for the bourbon glass to fly across the room. But that plane never left the hangar.Sam would give a startled look, genuinely surprised, and reply, "Oh! OK."

I would exhale in relief and watch to see if he just had a long fuse and the explosion was delayed. But after a moment, he'd light a cigarette as though it were his cue to start on another topic, completely forgetting he'd been yelled at less than a few minutes earlier. I was amazed that although they'd argue or trade one-liners, there was never any angry escalation or lingering animosity – let alone exchanged blows. They'd state the problem, forget it, and move on to the next topic that would be discussed just as vehemently. In all of those years, I never once heard them have one of the knock-down, drag-out pre-MMA fights that were my parents' norm. If I were a scientist, Pat and Sam would have been my Petri dish.

They both liked parties and entertained a lot. Their friends were as opinionated and well-read as they were, and no topic was off-limits. Pat and Sam argued just as vehemently with their friends as they did with each other and with the same lack of rancor. It was like a room full of New Yorkers arguing about the merits of the Yankees vs the Mets with the volume somewhat muted. Although the booze flowed as freely as it did with my alcoholic family, the discussions never grew into fights nor was there ever any sign of an escalation. It took some getting used to. The first few times that a lively discussion broke out, I felt my butt pucker as I sat on the edge of the leather couch on high alert. Legs tensed, in big sister mode, I was ready to grab Sammy out of bed at a moment's notice and hide him in the closet with me.

Although they could put the booze away, these people were nothing like my family. They were smart, witty, and sophisticated. They were cocktail drinkers who held shiny, clear glasses with olives or limes in them. My parents were strictly brown bottle Genesee beer drinkers. My mother claimed that hard liquor made people mean, so it wasn't allowed in the house. After a few parties with no flying fists, I started to relax. Pat and Sam's friends were actually quite nice, once I got used to them. They included me in their conversations and actually listened. I didn't come out of my shell right away, but I started to poke my head out.

Sam's friend Joe played honorary bartender one warm Saturday night. They seemed to take turns tending bar, although it was never clear to me how the role was filled. As if hearing a remote summons, either Pat, Sam, or one of the friends offered drinks and stuck with it for the remainder of the night. While Joe refilled glasses, I chatted with his wife, Norma, who had slightly protruding teeth and somewhat frizzy brown hair. I felt comfortable with her. She reminded me of our downstairs neighbor when I was in kindergarten.

Joe raised one of the clear glasses with ice in it. "Hey, Lor! Do you want a gin and tonic to cool off? We brought some fresh Rose's lime juice."

It was a beautiful night; the glow of the moon illuminated the patio through the open sliding glass doors. The Ohio Players grooved on the stereo and I was at a party with sophisticated people. A cold drink with lime would hit the spot. "Yeah! Sure! I'll take one."

Joe deftly mixed the tonic with Seagram's gin and added a quick splash of Rose's. His beefy hand passed the drink over to Norma. She put it on a coaster and slid it across the glass coffee table toward me.

I've heard that the first hit of crack cocaine is the best that high that anyone can imagine. Then it goes downhill after that initial high. Crack heads spend the rest of their lives as addicts futilely chasing a high that huge. I've never tried crack, but I have never had a better gin and tonic than the one that Joe made that night. With a single drink, I was on my way. The instant that alcohol lost the stigma that I had associated with beer-drinking losers, I was free to have a few cocktails. I still drew the line at beer, though. That shit had been my parent's downfall. Every single problem that existed in my family was due to Gennie and I would have none of it. I understood exactly how to manage alcohol: losers drank beer, winners drank cocktails. Not only did I feel like a sophisticated winner when I had a drink in one hand and a cigarette in the other, alcohol enabled me to be who I really was deep down inside: a party girl. Gin and tonic with lime was a magic elixir that did for me what I couldn't do for myself: it set me free. After a few drinks, I left myself behind and became the life of the party. Come out of my shell? Hell, I shot out of it like a cannon! I joked, I laughed, I flirted! Who knew life could be this much fun! If only my parents drank gin instead of beer, they wouldn't be so miserable!

Instead of dreading parties and social events, I started looking forward to them. I had many years of misery to make up for and intended to take advantage of every opportunity to do so. I discovered the impromptu parties that always sprung up in the barracks and started to join in the fun. We hung out in the barracks game room, shooting pool, playing air hockey, or just having a few drinks. I also found out that wine was a good substitute for gin for turning my party switch on. Wine still wasn't beer and it didn't require ice or a mixer; it was almost the perfect drink. Although we weren't supposed to keep booze in the barracks when we were in training, I started to stash a bottle or two of wine in my locker. One never knew when a party might break out and I didn't want to be left behind in case they only had beer. I wondered why no one else had ever made the beer = loser connection, but I was pretty damned proud of myself for figuring it out. Sometimes, especially after a few drinks, I almost couldn't stop congratulating myself on my cleverness.

I made a lot more friends since I'd found my inner party girl, and the more friends I made, the more parties I got invited to. It was an amazing phenomenon for a person who could barely hold a conversation six months earlier. I also started dating. Although the ratio of men to women was easily 30:1, I hadn't dated when I first arrived at Redstone. For some reason, it's difficult to date when you don't talk.

My dates were also my party pals, so our dates primarily consisted of going out to dinner and a few bars. It didn't take the guys long to figure out that I was a lot more fun when I was drinking, so we usually had a few drinks before we went out. Although I liked most of my dates well enough, I never felt anything more than that. I went out with them not only because I was so surprised that they asked me to, but also because I wanted to be like my aunt. She went on three or four dates a week for years, so surely there had to be something to it. To me, it was not unlike trying to like sports. I'd always seen people enjoying sports, and the players seemed to be having a good time, but I'd never understood the attraction. Why read a book at a game when you can read it at home where drinks are cheaper? The experience of dating men was not unlike going to a football game: everyone seemed to be having a good time except me. Like most people, I really liked the Hollywood happily-ever-after concept of love. I wasn't so sure about the marriage part, though – I didn't know many happily married people except for Sam and Pat, and the jury was still out on them.

As the ratio of men to women were stacked so heavily in my favor, I had my pick of guys to date. And since I had no clue what normal was, I leaned toward the unusual; I told myself that they wouldn't bore me as much. In retrospect, the ironies abounded: the shy, withdrawn girl who had barely dated in her life also wanted to ensure that she wasn't bored. It never once occurred to me that most people date because there is some type of attraction between them.

One shade shy of complete disassociation, I was dimly aware that I was attracted to women more than men, but, like many before me, concluded that I just hadn't met the right man yet.

Despite their quirkiness, the guys I dated were generally nice enough. None of them were violent, although one of them showed definite tendencies in that direction. I intuitively recognized the signs, and he didn't last long enough to settle into his wife-beating comfort level. Of course, every one of them had a drug or alcohol problem; I wouldn't have had any use for them otherwise. Since the competition for women was so stiff, the dates tended to get serious in short order. After celebrating our one month anniversary (if either of us were sober enough to remember), a proposal generally followed soon after. A pattern soon developed.

After the proposal, I'd take my fiancé over to Pat and Sam's so they could meet my future ex-husband. I'd come bounding in the door, nervous fiancé in hand. "Hi! This is my fiancé, Frank!"

Sam and Pat were civilized people, hospitable and gracious. We'd make small talk for an hour or so and I'd leave with Frank. Soon after drinks and dinner, I'd ditch him and go back to their house for a nightcap. "Well, what do you think of Frank?" I'd chirp.

Sam would light a cigarette, put both arms on the small bar, bow his head down between his arms and shake it back and forth slowly as though he'd just witnessed the most appallingly ridiculous thing he'd ever seen in his life.

As usual, Pat was more to the point. "No, Lor."

I was puzzled. I thought that they'd be happy for me. Their adopted daughter, married off so soon.

"I just don't see it, Lor," she added.

I didn't get angry; I didn't even defend the now-ex-fiancé and demand for them to give him a chance or even ask him to come back for dinner. It actually never occurred to me to ask why. I'd ditch Frank the next day and return back to Sam and Pat's in thirty days with the next fiancé du jour.

It took a while to figure out, but I realized later that Pat and Sam saw many things that I didn't: my total lack of affection (let alone love and passion) for the person that I'd barely met and was frivolously arranging to spend the rest of my life with. But most of all, they recognized my gay memo long before I did. They just stood by and let me whirl until I finally got it too.

CHAPTER NINE

1976

In addition to being my live demo for a normal family, Pat and Sam provided a rare added bonus, like a prize in a box of healthy cereal. They knew how to work within the college system, institutions that seemed like fortresses to me. Both were also from lower-middle-class families in Erie, and both had gotten their college degree while holding down a full-time job.

Pat had squeezed the college information out of me within the first five minutes that I was in her Cutlass that initial Sunday afternoon. "Why you be in the Army, mama?"

Pat channeled her inner Whoopi Goldberg long before Whoopi made it big. Perhaps she'd been Whoopi's role model. "I want to go to college on the G.I. Bill," I mumbled, staring out of the car window.

"Good plan. You can start taking classes as soon as you finish your Army training. The Army will pay for it while you're active duty so you won't have to dip into the G.I. Bill until you get out. You can probably take some classes on base. Sam finished his degree when we were stationed in Hawaii and I have a few more courses left. I've been taking classes since Christ was a fucking corporal."

I brightened considerably at this information. It never occurred to me to go to school and work at the same time.

We were at dinner one evening when she started in. "Please pass the gravy. Hey, when are you going to sign up for some courses, mama?" She had just passed one of her finals that day and I thought that the topic had just occurred to her. Little did I know that Pat was like a pit bull with lockjaw once an idea took up residence in her head. I was to hear that same question from her for the next fourteen years until I finally showed her my diploma.

"I want to finish training classes first. I need to score high enough to get a promotion when I graduate, and these last couple of classes are kicking my ass." Those with the top three overall scores in the class were eligible for promotion upon graduation, and I was currently in second place. A promotion meant a raise, which might mean I could afford to get an apartment off-post. I had a simple motive for moving off post: the ability to smoke pot with impunity and ensure that the MPs didn't bust me in the barracks. I'd developed a real appetite for gin and tonic with lime, but just like Jell-O, there was always room for pot.

"The winter term starts in January and you haven't even applied yet," she informed me as she lit a Benson and Hedges. "It will take a couple of months to get the paperwork rolling. Go sign up this week."

She didn't suggest that I do it, she didn't indicate that it might be a good idea that I do it. Just do it. No discussion needed. Do it now. Pat would have made a great First Sergeant. But I was embarrassed to tell my personal First Sergeant that I had no idea how to start the admittance process; she wasn't a big fan of excuses.

Fortunately, she continued on as though she'd read my mind. "The Education Office on post will have all of the paperwork to get the ball rolling and it won't cost you a dime." Like any good Army sergeant, she had just kicked all of the legs out from under my excuses.

Around the same time, I was lounging during a smoke break in Pershing class one hot day in October. It was still Indian summer in Alabama. A bunch of us were hanging outside the school building, drinking cokes and lighting one cigarette from another before we went back to class. As we leaned against the outside of the large metal building that housed the Pershing launchers and computer classes, we were approached by an old black sergeant. I'd seen him before, a Sergeant First Class with shoulders permanently hunched over as though he'd been slouching at a desk for most of his life. He shuffled around the classroom area a lot, but I had no idea who he was nor had I ever heard anyone speak of him. I assumed that he was with the cleanup crew – he just didn't appear as arrogant as most of the NCOs. It never dawned on me that we, the students, were the cleanup crew. Blowing smoke rings, I watched him make a beeline for me, never sparing a glance for anyone else.

He stopped directly in front of me and looked me in the eye. Through my peripheral vision, I noted that his uniform was starched perfectly. His shiny boots were more spit shined than mine, no mean feat. I considered myself the champion of spit polished boots since I shined them every night for hours after I got stoned. He looked down on the ground at me as I sprawled against the building, sunlight reflecting off his perspiring, bald, black head.

"Frombach?" He had a deep voice, probably like the one that Moses had heard booming out at him.

I eyed him lazily as I took a drag on the smoke. "Yeah?"

"Stand when I'm talking to you, soldier!"

My coke spilled and I dropped the cigarette in amazement, coughing from the menthol smoke stuck in my lungs. I rose from the ground like one of the Pershing rockets had gone off in my ass. The name on his uniform said Holmes. "Yes, Sergeant Holmes. My apologies, Sergeant." I stifled the urge to call him sir, but only officers were called sir. Demonstrating a lack of military protocol would just piss him off even more.

"Follow me."

I couldn't imagine what in the hell he could want with me. Did I need to clean something up? The class went everywhere together, like lemmings or prisoners. Why didn't my classmates have to police the area or clean up as well? I resisted the overwhelming urge to whine about it.

He marched me about fifty yards away from the group. Then he turned and spoke to me softly in a voice as smooth and deep as a fine southern bourbon, a marked difference from his previous bark. "Do you know who I am?"

"No, Sergeant."

"I'm Sergeant Holmes. I'm in charge of the equipment repair crew here at the school, and I've been watching you."

I gaped, speechless. What could I have done wrong?

"I see that you're a hard worker, and I've spoken with your instructors. They say you're smart. Now you're going to graduate soon. You're scheduled to go over to the maintenance depot, where they'll turn you into a clerk and you'll push papers for the next two years. I can offer you an alternative. You can come to work for me and actually perform the job that you've just trained for. I'll make you work, but you'll actually learn something. I can get your orders changed, but it's up to you. Choose."

Had the Matrix movie series been released by then, I would have felt like Neo with Morpheus in front of him, red pill in one hand, blue pill in the other. In the movie, Morpheus explains, "You take the blue pill – the story ends, you wake up in your bed and believe whatever you want to believe. You take the red pill – you stay in Wonderland, and I show you how deep the rabbit hole goes." Choose, Neo.

Neo took a few minutes to choose the red pill. I took nowhere near that long. I looked Sergeant Holmes dead in the eye and said, "I'm in."

Sergeant Holmes nodded his head. "All right, then." He shuffled away without another word, head bowed down between slumped shoulders.

Sergeant Holmes was true to his word and then some. As it turned out, his crew was already overstaffed. He needed another troop in his crew like he needed more starch in his uniform. I was the only woman in the crew and he cut me no breaks because of it, but he did give something I'd never had before: opportunity. I'd been working in his crew for about a month when he called me aside again.

"I want you to start getting ready to compete for Soldier of the Month. I think you can do it."

"What's that?"

"It's a competition. You have to memorize the study guide, look sharp, and go before a board. It would help if you start taking correspondence courses. They like to see initiative. I'll work with you on practicing how to act in front of the board."

I gaped again. A man that I'd never heard of a couple of months ago was making of habit of rendering me speechless. "OK."

He gave me a sharp look. "What did you say?"

This time I had the grace to be embarrassed. "Yes, Sergeant Holmes."

I pushed my application for the local junior college out for another semester while I studied for the board. I took correspondence courses during breaks at work and studied the military trivia handbook after a joint or two at night. I told myself that the pot helped me concentrate. I wasn't particularly interested in drinking because I was too busy to go out. Booze was only for social occasions. Sergeant Holmes walked me through mock boards and told me exactly what to expect and how to answer the questions.

"They're going to ask you the questions exactly as they are in the manual. They expect the exact answers. If you can't remember right away, ask them to repeat the question. Think hard for the answer during the time that they're repeating the question. Sometimes a few extra seconds will help." It wouldn't be the only lesson that Sergeant Holmes would teach me that I would use on many other occasions throughout the rest of my life.

With Sergeant Holmes coaching, I made Battalion Soldier of the Month and subsequently, Soldier of the Year. It was the first time in my life that I'd achieved anything and it was a high that even drugs and alcohol couldn't touch. I thought that my parents would be as apathetic toward my awards as they were toward everything else. Unfortunately, I was wrong. Their reaction was much worse. I called my mother to tell her the good news. At that time, I was still very conflicted about her. I hated her, but she was still my mother and I wanted her to be proud of me.

"Guess what? I made Soldier of the Year!"

"That's my kid," she gushed.

I was stunned. "What did you say?" Was she really proud of me? Did the universe just tilt on its axis?

"See how well I taught you? You're a chip off the old block."

How in the hell had she turned my accomplishment into her own? "You never made Soldier of the Year."

"No, but you're my kid. That's how you did it. It's how you I raised you." She almost broke her arm patting herself on the back.

I slammed the pay phone down in a blind rage; my excitement had turned to rage in a nanosecond. Some things never changed. Fuck her. I needed a drink.

CHAPTER TEN

1978

Although I'd learned a lot in the Army, three years was enough. I'd packed a lot into that time. Not only had I begun to understand that not all families are toxic and that I could actually accomplish something when all of my emotional bandwidth wasn't consumed coping with my malignant relatives, but the ticking time bomb of my own alcoholism had been ignited and I'd gradually realized that I was gay.

Once I'd lost my fear of alcohol, I embraced booze and parties with all the fervor of the newly converted. Like most recent converts, my life surrounded my new obsession and drinking became my Alpha and my Omega, my lover and my best friend, all rolled into one lovely liquid. Someone once described heroin as a big, warm hug delivered through a needle; I felt the same way about alcohol and I wanted to be hugged all of the time. I liked drugs well enough, but never found a drug that did it for me like alcohol did. No damn wonder my parents drank. Why didn't they tell me it was so awesome? I didn't realize that alcohol doesn't affect normal people that way. When most people begin to feel the effects of a drink, they stop. They often say, "No, thanks. I don't want another drink. I'm beginning to feel it." For us alcoholics, that feeling is exactly what we're looking for. After those few drinks, at the point when most people begin to feel out of control, we drunks believe that we're starting to feel *in* control. And, like many alcoholics, I quickly got to the point where I didn't care what I drank to feel the effects of that warm hug. I remember the first time I drank a beer and was surprised to discover that I wasn't revolted. I was completely aware that I'd just had a beer after years of despising my parents for their disgusting addiction to Gennie, but I still didn't take it as a sign that I was falling further down the rabbit hole. On the contrary, I actually smiled to myself and took it as yet another sign of my superiority; the beer was "only" Miller Light, a far cry from Genesee Cream Ale, at least in my mind. The first lie alcoholics tell is the one we tell to ourselves.

I went to a lot of parties at my barrack sergeant's apartment. Ironically, although she was the ranking non-commissioned officer (NCO) in the women's barracks, she lived off-post with her girlfriend. Jane was an attractive blonde who made no secret of the fact that she was a lesbian, and it hadn't hurt her Army career one bit. At the time, none of the brass at Redstone cared who anyone slept with, as long as you did your job. Although we lived off-post, we were both considered single by Army standards and therefore had to maintain a room in the barracks and assist with barracks cleaning. Jane came in several times a week to inspect the rooms and ensure that the area met Army cleanliness standards. It turned out that we enjoyed each other's sense of humor so she began inviting me to their parties.

I didn't go to every party that she invited me to, but went more often than not. On those occasions, I never took a boyfriend with me, although Jane made it clear that I was welcome to bring whomever I wanted. I told myself it was because I hadn't seen any other men at her house and didn't want my boyfriend du jour to feel uncomfortable. Then, one Saturday afternoon, Jane called me aside after an all-morning cleaning "party" in preparation for a Monday morning barracks inspection by the Inspector General (IG).

"Close the door," she said as I walked into her large, bright room at the end of the hallway. As the ranking NCO, Jane was entitled to the largest room with a lot of windows, and it was the only one that included a private bathroom.

"What's all the mystery about? Is there a big secret?" I asked in a joking stage whisper.

"Come over here and sit down." She patted a spot on the woolen green blanket covering her bunk. An engineering type even back then, I mentally noted that since she'd sat on it, she'd have to tighten up the perfectly made bunk before the inspection. The IG could have been one of those old-fashioned Army types that still wanted to see a bed made so tightly that a quarter bounced when it was flipped on the blanket. I plopped down next to her.

"Is everything OK?" I was concerned, as she wasn't smiling. Jane almost always had a smile on her face.

"No. Yes. Well, not really." She stared out toward the sun-drenched marching field that her window overlooked. Now I was really anxious; this wasn't the Jane that I knew at all. I sat silently, waiting for her to continue. I could feel the itchy wool of the blanket through my fatigues. After a few minutes, her head turned back toward me, with what seemed to be an enormous effort.

"Why don't you ever bring Jim with you to my house?" she asked. Jim was my current boyfriend.

"What? I don't know. I guess because there's no reason to. There aren't any other guys there."

"Is there another reason?" Her eyes were now boring into mine. Uncomfortable and confused, I looked away and then looked back at her. Our eyes met and it finally dawned on me what was going on.

"No! What are you talking about?" Although I was pretty sure that I knew.

"Is it because you don't like men? That you're really like me?" She was speaking so softly that I had to strain to hear her.

"Absolutely not! You know me! I just like to party and have a good time!" I knew that I should get up from Jane and her itchy blanket and run out into the freshly waxed hallway, but I stayed. A part of me knew that she was right. I enjoyed drinking with my boyfriends, but didn't enjoy much else with them, including sex. I just assumed that I hadn't met the right one yet. But I was intrigued when I was with the women at Jane's and felt comfortable there in a way that I hadn't anywhere else; I just couldn't admit it.

"Are you sure?" Then she leaned in and gently kissed me. It wasn't like any kiss that I'd ever felt before. With men, kissing was a necessary first base on their way to the home run, and they all spent as much time on it as they would on first base if the ball had gone into the stands. I also would have bet that they were more skilled at rounding bases than they were at kissing. But Jane was different, she was skilled and in no hurry. I almost stopped breathing and my heart was beating so fast that I thought it would burst.

After a few minutes, she leaned back and smiled. "You're a great kisser. Too bad that you're wasting your talent on Jim!"

"What about your girlfriend?" I was all kinds of confused.

"She doesn't have to know. We can just meet here at the barracks."

I shook my head. "No. That won't work for me." I finally gave in to my urge to get up and flee.

I ran into my own room and slammed the door. I strode over to the full-length mirror and looked at myself. I didn't look like a lesbian. With the exception of Jane, all of the gay women that I'd seen looked like they played butch or femme, and I didn't want to be either one. I just wanted to be me, whatever that was. I felt so comfortable with the lesbians, yet I couldn't picture myself dressing the way that they did...but I also couldn't see myself enduring Jim or anyone like him for one more minute. I was in a sexual identity DMZ. I looked at myself again and started to cry.

I broke up with Jim that weekend, but I never went back to Jane's, nor did I ever speak to her again. As it turned out, she eventually left her girlfriend and found a boyfriend. A few months later, I took my honorable discharge and set out to make my fortune in the computer industry. Although I immediately got a great job, it turned out that while I *thought* I wanted a computer job, what I *really* wanted was a computer company to pay me to get drunk and high. As a civilian, my budget was a lot higher than it had been in the Army, so I could afford to drink a lot more and buy more expensive drugs. If you do that a lot, you may soon decide that partying is more important than a regular income. You also won't have an issue getting your boss to agree to echo Charles Grodin's sentiment: It would be so nice if you weren't here. So I left the job to focus on partying, and life was good while the money held out.

Unsurprisingly, getting that loaded so often tends to fuck up your decision-making ability. Less than three years after I lost my fear of alcohol and less than a year after I got out of the Army, I came out of a semi-blackout and found myself in Santa Rosa, California. Fueled by a potent cocktail of hormones, LSD, and Miller Light, I'd followed someone that I met at a party out to the small town near San Francisco. Unfortunately, this person was already in a relationship, which she neglected to mention in the couple of weeks that we knew each other. Since I'd spent what little savings I had on a Greyhound ticket and dope for the bus ride, I came out of the blackout in a strange city with no money, no job, and nowhere to live. Far from my days as Soldier of the Year, I'd essentially become a stoned version of Blanche Dubois: arriving in a new town penniless, with no thought for the morrow and dependent upon the kindness of strangers.

Eventually I wound up in a bar with my party pal and her girlfriend. The pal didn't quite know what to do with me since she'd gotten back together with her gal, so we went to the bar. We just knew that a few drinks would somehow resolve the awkward situation with the three of us, and it did. That bar is where I ran into Chamomile. In the late 70s, Northern California was the epicenter of women's consciousness-raising and communal living, and Chamomile had turned her house into such a community. In retrospect, it was probably not unlike a pet adoption event where you threaten to take the puppy to the pound if no one adopts it. Sooner or later, some compassionate schmuck will step forward, or at least stay put while everyone else steps back. Everyone else stepped back while Cam was out back blowing off a joint, so she got stuck adopting me. She really didn't have to, of course, but she was a kind soul who was into the sisterhood and was more than slightly stoned.

I dimly discerned through my own cannabis fog that Cam lived with a number of other people, although nobody came right out and called it a commune. They preferred the term "female collective". Although I had no idea what that meant, she described the women's movement in Marxist terms so passionately that I found myself mirroring the fierce look on her face and solemnly nodding my head in agreement. Children of alcoholics are chameleons and I could blend in with the best of them, even in the strange land of California.

"We're tired of being weighed down by male patrician capitalism!" Cam screamed, trying to make her political point heard over the noise of the bar.

"Right on!" I screamed right back at her. I was more capitalist than socialist, but it didn't seem quite the right time to bring that up.

"From each according to their ability, to each according to their needs." She was obviously enamored with Marx.

When the bar closed and Cammy invited me to join her commune, I hugged the only two people I knew in the state goodbye and joined my new roommate in a beat-up Chevy Impala to ride to her house. The ludicrousness of moving in with a complete stranger never once occurred to me. I was an old hand at it by then. After all, I'd just followed someone I barely knew across the country.

On the ride to her house, Cam mentioned that the community consisted of least three people but usually not more than five on any given day. As we pulled up in front of her home, it occurred to me that it more fit the description of a bungalow than a house, but whenever we talked about it, it was obvious that it was The House. Capital T, Capital H.

Chamomile semi-dragged me into The House and laid out my choices. "You can sleep in my room, with these womyn on the floor, or there's a bed in the back porch that nobody's using right now."

I nodded my head in the direction of what I hoped was the back of the house. No Stanley Kowalski, she shrugged a shoulder, told me to be careful climbing, and padded off to bed in bare feet that hadn't had more than a nodding acquaintanceship with shoes in years. In most civilizations, including the planet of California, if a person rescues your ass from being homeless, you really should demonstrate your gratitude. And if you're flat-out broke without even a phone-call dime, there is only one currency left: sex. Cammy's seemingly altruistic gesture of rescuing me was probably based more on an expectation that I would demonstrate my gratitude rather than giving a rat's ass whether or not a stray sister wandered the streets – consciousness-raising and sisterhood notwithstanding. But my gratitude boiled down to a barely mumbled thank you. I really would rather have slept on the street than have sex with Chamomile. The poor thing carried unattractiveness to a whole new level. Although I couldn't have afforded to be picky, and 70s Marxist feminists weren't supposed to be shallow enough to care about outward appearances, I just couldn't.

Feminist lesbians of that time were the antithesis of male-dominated stereotypes and could prove it. Wo-men translated to: Whoa, men and all of your bullshit male values. Hair shaved short or really long and braided, unfashionable hair was a metaphor for the movement: you were pro-women or pro-men, there was no middle ground. Being pro-women meant no shaving. No washing. Wearing thrift store clothes. Worn Army fatigues with peace symbols and American flags sewn upside down. Peace. Sister. Olivia records. Womyn. Love. Wimmin. Whoa, men.

Cammy was no nouveau feminist and carried her braided, unwashed, unshaved self proudly. If I had been more into consciousness-raising at the time, maybe even the least bit feminist or a lot less shallow, I might have been able to look past Cam's rough exterior and provide gratitude – or, at the very least, a pity fuck. However, I was far more into losing consciousness than raising it, a trait that would persist for many years. I was unable to find my rescuer attractive, and I couldn't get high enough or drunk enough to sleep with any of the others, either. When the chips were down, it turned out that I was more bourgeoisie than proletariat after all.

The only light on in the house was toward the back, so I staggered in that direction. Passing a sparsely furnished dining room, I entered a small kitchen. Of course, it smelled of pot; that was to be expected. But one of the sisters was a big fan of patchouli incense as well. A small light bulb without a globe cast a slightly yellow glow over the sink and I could see that the kitchen was surprisingly clean and orderly. Fortunately, their lack of cleanliness seemed to apply only to personal hygiene and not the common areas. Not that I should have cared...my options were limited. Still, this beggar was definitely choosey.

An open door off to the left revealed the small bathroom, leaving a single closed door which appeared to lead to the porch. It opened easily to reveal what appeared to be a very tall bunk bed minus the bottom bunk. Cammie's comment about the climb now made sense. A bunch of junk was piled where the bottom bunk would have been. Illuminated by the small kitchen light, the contraption looked like a homemade crib for a baby giant. The bunk was as tall as I was and there was no ladder. I made several weak tries to climb up the supporting slats in the front of the frame, but couldn't overcome gravity with the booze and drugs addling my balance. So I gave up after a few weak attempts and passed out on the bare wooden floor.

I slowly drifted back to consciousness. Rough sand rained lightly on my face and bare arms, and the floor felt like sandpaper. I had no idea where in the hell I'd wound up. What the fuck had I gotten myself into this time? I vaguely remembered the previous night. I seemed to remember a giant crib, but wasn't sure whether it had been a dream. When I'd started blacking out a couple of years earlier, I developed the practice of never opening my eyes without first trying to remember what had happened the night before, as I never knew where I was going to end up. Sometimes I would find myself coming to in a strange bed, my car, a golf course with sprinklers going, or who knows where else. The possibilities were becoming endless as my drinking progressed. The trick was to assemble whatever puzzle pieces were available and to rationalize the pieces that were missing or out of place. If the pieces aren't there, make 'em up. Some people wonder why alcoholics and addicts constantly lie. It's a habit that we've acquired from long practice of first and foremost lying to ourselves. We don't call it lying, of course; we're just filling in the missing pieces as we'd like for them to be. After a while, the fine line between fact and fiction becomes a wide, hazy DMZ.

Eyes still closed, I couldn't imagine where the loose sand was coming from or why I had fallen asleep on sandpaper. As my mind gingerly pushed the fog away, I felt the sharp tip of the hangover spear behind my temple. The Sahara in my mouth felt as gritty as the sandpaper on my face. Through my sensory information-gathering exercise, I dimly became aware of a soft mewing. Curiosity bested my memory scan of the previous night and I slowly opened one eye as a beta test. Sunlight clanged throughout my head, giving every cell a painful command to attention. Front and center, Frombach. I immediately slammed the eye shut again, returning to blissful darkness. My brain would need a minute to recharge its defenses. Shore up the sandbags for another daylight assault.

"Damn," I thought. For someone without a cent to their name, I'd sure managed to get loaded enough to have a supernova hangover. Another low groan. Not mine, although it certainly felt like it. Barely audible, but definitely there. Taking a deep breath, I forced my eye open again to take stock of my surroundings. I slowly raised my head and looked around. I'd fallen asleep on the only floor covering there was: an old straw welcome mat. I was in the enclosed porch, but whoever worked on the enclosure project had run out of money or interest to finish the job on the flooring. Riding another deep breath to prepare for the onslaught of pain, I slowly sat up. The hangover spear settled into my brain a little deeper as I took a better look around.

The porch was the store room for my new roommates and obviously a number of their old roommates. I hadn't just imagined the giant crib. Underneath it, dusty boxes and filled garbage bags were scattered everywhere like a storage unit had exploded a long time ago and no one had come along to clean it up. I stood up very slowly. Still getting my hangover sea legs, I lurched forward a few steps to examine the strange bunk crib. Another wail. Carefully moving disintegrating boxes and dusty Life magazines, I uncovered a litter of four tiny kittens in a pile of old clothes. Their eyes were open, but they were so tiny...they could be little more than two weeks old. Their little mouths were in constant motion, trying to nurse on something, anything. I was afraid to touch them. At any moment, a mama cat could shoot out of the debris and attach her claws to my face. It didn't occur to me that if their mother were around, they wouldn't have been so hungry. Nature imbues her four-legged creatures with stronger maternal instincts than many that walk upright.

Hangover almost forgotten, I sat down on a yellowing box to slowly get a little closer. As I got a better look at the kittens, I noticed that something wasn't quite right. They looked strange. I couldn't figure out what it was for a moment. When I did, I thought that last night's buzz was still affecting my vision. Weirdly, their tiny fur seemed to be in motion. Still under the threat of mama cat claws, I tentatively edged even closer. When I realized what I was seeing, I wished that I had not. Horror struck as I realized that there was indeed motion on the kittens, a lot of it. They were covered with fleas, thousands of fleas. I then realized that the sand I felt on my face wasn't sand at all – the parasites had quickly migrated to the new buffet passed out on the welcome mat.

I ran into the house, past the snoring sisters on the floor. Flinging Cammie's bedroom door open, I screamed at the lump under the covers, trying to remember her name. "Tammie, Tammie! There's a litter of kittens on the porch! They're covered in fleas! They're really hungry. Where's the mother? Can we do something?" The words came out machine-gun style: RAT-TAT-TAT-TAT-TAT.

Cam shot straight up at the ruckus and so did the women on the floor. Bare breasts of all sizes and shapes flopped with the sudden motion.

"Holy shit!"

"What the fuck?"

"Damn, what's goin' on, woman?"

"What's happenin'?"

If this had been a rock opera, they would have been the chorus. Fixated on the queen bee, I ignored the chorus line and their heaving breasts.

Cam threw herself back down on a pile of pillows that would have made Cleopatra proud. There was obviously a lot of scrimping going on in the small house, but not in the pillow department. Her room was decorated as though she'd expected Stevie Nicks to go lesbo and arrive any moment. Antique lamps covered with lacy shawls and a soft gauze tent over the bed made up a much softer décor than I would have expected from this hard-core Amazon. Her response to my announcement belied the tone of the room and surprised me, considering she had just saved my ass from being homeless the night before.

"Jesus Christ," Cammie spat. "What the fuck? You're all excited about that shit? They're fine. They've been there a couple weeks or so. The mother runs around outside a lot. She'll come back when she's ready, probably this morning. She's a whore cat. And my name isn't Tammie."

Still excited, I wasn't ready to let go that easily. "But it doesn't look like they've eaten in a while. And, they're covered, covered with fleas! I had fleas on me!"

In no mood for anything besides sleep, Cam rolled back over and waved me away. A dark patch of fur was visible from her unshaven armpit as she raised her arm to hasten me on my way.

Dismissed, I slunk past the gaggle of women that had just woken. They were surprisingly good-natured and didn't bitch about the interruption. Like Cammie, they also intended to sleep through the better part of the day and rolled over to finish the task. Left to my own devices, I found some milk in the refrigerator. I then headed for the bathroom to hunt down an eyedropper and found success in the form of Neo-Synephrine, the runny nose remedy. Rinsing the nose dropper and heating the milk, I was armed for makeshift kitten rescue. A small, pale woman with slightly bleary eyes wearing nothing but light grey sweatpants came out to go to the bathroom just as I was taking the pan of milk off of the stove.

"What are you doing?" she inquired, one eyebrow slightly raised. She knew damn well that the milk didn't belong to me, but I had no idea if it was hers, or whether looting food mattered to the collective.

"I borrowed some milk," I babbled, nervous that she would throw me out on the street for milk theft. "I thought it might help the kittens."

"They'll be fine," she assured me, just like Cam had. "But it can't hurt to give them a snack. Just make sure that you leave enough for Linda's coffee. She gets cranky if she has to drink it black." She gave me a slight smile and continued to the bathroom.

Relieved, I went back to the porch to try the feeding experiment. The kittens actually scared me. Since I knew that the mother cat was gone, I was no longer afraid of getting of my face clawed off, but the kittens themselves weren't normal. Kittens are supposed to be so cute and cuddly that your heart just melts, but there was nothing snuggly about these poor, weird creatures. The mother must have been gone longer than the sisters thought, because these baby kitties really didn't seem like cats at all. They were like nothing I'd ever seen, more alien than feline. When they tried to walk, they lacked the graceful motion that defines the species. Instead, they were jerky and spastic as though their limbs were being remotely controlled by a toddler. Their tiny eyes constantly darted back forth as though frantically searching for something. Hissing and lurching, they cried continually.

As it turned out, the mother cat never returned. Without an adult to provide a role model, the kittens had no idea of how to be a cat. It seemed as though their internal mechanisms were aware that something was terribly wrong, with no idea of how to make it right. Not surprisingly, they died a couple of days later. Those kittens still haunt me. For years afterward, I would wake up in the middle of the night to see their tiny, freakish faces flash in my mind's eye. It took a long time to figure out that my insides mirrored the aliens looking outside of those lost, lurching little souls.

CHAPTER ELEVEN

1979

I only lasted a few months in the commune. I'd found some odd jobs so that I could contribute toward my keep, but nothing steady...and I refused to get food stamps, as that would mean that I had become my mother incarnate. Gertie obtained food stamps as soon as she could after the divorce. For a long time, she still couldn't bring herself to leave the house to go grocery shopping so I would go for her when Beth was working. Inevitably she demanded a Delmonico steak for dinner, and I refused to look at the clerks as they rung up the expensive cut of meat while I counted out the food stamps. Finally, Bumpy offered to wire me a bus ticket back to Erie and I took it. It took four days to get from California to Pennsylvania, and I didn't have any drugs to make this trip more bearable. My grandfather included an extra twenty-five dollars in the Western Union money order with the caveat that I use it for meals. Since I was headed back home, I knew I needed a drink more than food, so I split the difference and used half for meals and half for beer. Neither went far enough, but lack of food made the beer go a whole lot further. My grandfather also made it clear that although he would lend me enough for the trip, room and board wouldn't be included in the deal. Since I had nowhere else to live, my only option was my mother's house. There wasn't enough beer in the world to make that prospect tolerable.

Settling back in to life in Erie, I hooked up with some of my old drinking and drugging pals. They would always be good for a few drinks or tokes. One hot August day, I sat with my friend Jan as we waited for her father to get out of work. Lighting a cigarette, I habitually cupped my hand around the match head to shield the flame from the wind. It was a futile gesture in this case, as there hadn't been a breeze off the lake in weeks. Cool menthol eased slowly down my throat like a lazy serpent and I flicked the burnt match out of the open passenger side window. It was unseasonably hot, and like most cars of that time, the old Marquis was a stranger to air conditioning. Shifting slightly in the seat so that my t-shirt could absorb the sweat slowly trickling down the center of my back, I thought that if hell is an inferno served up with a side of sheer monotony, I had surely crossed the river Styx. Although the boredom bothered me far more than the heat, I was in no mood for either one. Even in summer, any day that isn't cold and gloomy in Erie is a bonus. But given my druthers, I would have taken the bonus somewhere else. I exhaled the smoke out of the window and turned toward my friend, Jan.

"What time does he usually get out?" I asked.

Neither of us had a car, so Jan had borrowed her father's ancient Marquis for the day so that we could run some errands. Waiting for him to get out of work was the downside of the deal. Her father, Gary, worked for the maintenance department of the local college and could have gotten caught up in a last-minute repair. On the other hand, he'd never been introduced to promptness and today probably wouldn't be the day for the introduction.

The brown interior of the aged classic had held up surprisingly well, like a Broadway actress with good genes and a reliable plastic surgeon. But the sagging exterior bore battle scars of every endured Pennsylvania winter. The shocks were shot, and the fenders and doors were pockmarked with fiberglass and Bondo, wistful bandages against PennDoT's road salt and its wicked child, corrosive rust. Gary was frugal and insisted on driving the thing despite the fact that he could have afforded better. I hoped that no one I knew would happen by and see me in the rust bucket.

Jan lit her cigarette from mine and took a deep drag. "He's supposed to get out at three-thirty, but you know how he is. Who knows? Maybe something came up."

That something could have been anything from a flustered professor with a stopped sink to the allure of the corner bar. I hoped it wasn't the bar as I was looking to stop for a couple of beers on the way home and I knew he'd be good for the tab. If he'd already had a couple of boilermakers, I'd be out of luck. I'd just gotten back from the commune a few weeks ago and was still broke. I was cashing in pop bottles for cigarette money and mooching drinks where I could get them. My grand scheme was to hang out in Erie for a month or so until I could get a job in a big city like Cleveland or Pittsburgh and then get the hell out again. It was an ambitious plan for someone with no money, let alone a car. It was also a plan that was as short on details as it was long on ambition. When you got right down to it, I had no idea what in the hell I was going to do.

We sat in the parking lot across from the college and smoked in silence. I glanced around idly. I hadn't seen downtown Erie in daylight in years. I noticed that the old fraternity house over on Sassafras Street had been demolished. The gaping, bare lot where it stood provided yet another addition to the blight of the aging city. It would be several years before the crack cocaine epidemic would turn the downtown into a full-bore war zone, but the battleground was already being staged by lack of funding and a corrupt city government.

As I looked around the parking lot littered with potholes still unrepaired from the previous winter, I berated myself silently. How in the hell had I wound up back here? I thought that I'd escaped this shithole for good, how did I wind up right where I started? I'd managed to run my life back into the ground in just a few short years. I shook my head at my own stupidity and tossed the cigarette butt out of the window. Who cared? I'd be outta here before I knew it.

"Do you want to see if we can find him?" I asked hopefully. Maybe we could track him down to the bar and I'd get those free beers after all.

Jan shook her head. "Nah. He'll show up soon enough."

Trying to hide my impatience, I opened the door and got out of the car to stretch. Behind the car, there was an office building with a big IBM sign in white letters on the glass door. I vaguely remembered that IBM had something to do with computers.

I leaned in the car window. "Hey, I'm gonna walk over to that office building for a sec, be right back."

Jan shrugged. "OK. Don't be gone long. He'll be pissed if he has to wait."

"I know the feeling," I said, more to myself than to her. A Type-A personality in all circumstances, I was incensed at any delay. Despite the fact that I had nowhere to go and all day to get there, waiting drove me nuts. As I walked up to the spotless glass door of the IBM office building, I caught a glimpse of myself in the reflection – commune-style comrade haircut, chopped off jean shorts, tight red t-shirt and a women's lib chest that refused to be restrained by a bra. I briefly considered returning at another time, dressed more appropriately. But I reminded myself that I was pretty much wearing my entire wardrobe, so it wouldn't have made any difference. Brass balls a-clanking, I opened the door and went in.

I got a job application from the IBM receptionist who provided the form with much more politeness than my commune costume deserved. I sent it in and received a call a few days later from the IBM Field Manager for an interview. My grandfather lent me another fifty dollars to buy a three-piece interview slacks suit and Beth lent me a pair of her good shoes.

On the day of the interview, I came downstairs into the living room wearing my new suit. Fifteen-year-old Mary Pat was sitting on the couch, reading a book. She glanced up from her paperback as I walked in and grimaced.

"Hey, how do I look?" I asked her. I felt weird. I hadn't dressed up for work since my typing pool days.

"Where's your shirt?" she asked, grimace still on her face. I was wearing a grey charcoal suit with a blue corduroy vest and nothing else.

"What do you mean, where's my shirt? I have a vest on, I'm decent." I was honestly puzzled. Still in commune-mode, it never occurred to me that the rest of the world might be operating on a slightly different dress code frequency, let alone corporate America.

"Stay here. Do not walk out that door. You can't walk around Erie looking like that, especially to an interview." Mary threw her book down on the couch and ran upstairs. She ran back down a few seconds later with a white blouse in one hand and a black purse in the other. She shoved the blouse at me and started stuffing newspaper into the purse so that it looked as though it had something in it.

"Go put this on and take the purse with you. Don't open it in front of anyone or they'll think you're weirder than you are. I wish you had some makeup on, but there's no time."

I gave up the fight and quickly put the blouse on. "If I miss the bus because of this damn blouse, I'm kicking your ass."

Mary rolled her eyes and tossed me the purse. I caught it and ran out the door.

The blouse and newspaper-filled purse worked their magic and I went to work as an IBM Customer Service Representative, repairing corporate computers. The only caveat was that IBM wanted me in Erie. Welcome home, kiddo. IBM sentenced me to the Erie gulag for seven winters.

During those seven years there was the occasional drunk drama with my parents that I would ignore as long as possible, hoping that someone else would take care of their shit. Sometimes I lucked out, other times my luck ran out. One night, I rolled snake eyes when I answered the phone after work.

"I'm having a heart attack," my father moaned.

As soon as I heard his voice on the phone, I knew where this was going. "Call 911." I rolled my eyes at my girlfriend, Darla, and then took a large swallow of my gin and tonic. I motioned for her to add more gin.

"The ambulance will cost too much."

"What do you want me to do?" I asked rhetorically. I knew what was coming. I closed my eyes and put the cold glass up to my forehead, waiting for the whiner to get to the point.

"Come down and take me to the emergency room."

"I can't. Call 911," I repeated. Beth was either out or not answering the phone. He usually hit her up first, as he could count on her to be nice. He knew better with me.

"I'm dying. Please take me to the hospital. Please."

I hung up.

Having overhead the last sentence, Darla gaped at me. "Jesus Christ. Your father is dying and you won't take him to the hospital?"

"Nope. He isn't dying. He's drunk." I lit a Kool Mild and sat down at the kitchen table and poured myself another drink.

"You can be one cold bitch. If you won't take him, I will. I'm not sitting by and letting your father die."

I started laughing, pissing her off even more. I said, "OK. Let's go play ambulance. But we're taking your car; I don't want him puking in mine."

We got in her orange Honda Civic and Dar drove like a bat out of hell, convinced that she was personally standing between my father and the Angel of Death. Darla had been a medic in the Army and more than likely pictured herself as a caring Hawkeye Pierce; the only voice of reason in a deadly family war zone. I was an ignoramus who couldn't be counted on to support the troops in their time of need. When we arrived at my father's small apartment twenty minutes later, I tossed back the last of the gin before we got out of the car. As we walked toward his apartment, I laughed out loud.

"I'll bet you twenty bucks that the asshole is drunk!"

"Go fuck yourself," she said flatly. "I can't believe that you're talking about your own father like this."

"Fifty! Make it fifty!" I could hardly contain myself. She shook her head at my callousness.

I pushed the doorbell in the middle of his apartment door and he opened it immediately, as though he were waiting on the other side. He looked like hell; his short, grey hair was greasy and unwashed and he hadn't shaved in days. But his bloodshot eyes told me everything I needed to know. He leaned against the doorjamb for support, barely able to breathe. He reeked of whiskey.

"C'mon in. Lemme jus' grab my keys." He could barely get the words out.

I pushed past him into the meticulously tidy apartment. One thing I could say for him, he was the neatest drunk I'd ever seen. They must have been OCD at the orphanage. No wonder he used to have a conniption fit at the eternal towel pile on the couch.

"It looks like you've been drinking." I couldn't resist. I turned toward my girlfriend and smirked. She gaped at him as he lurched around like an unhinged hunchback of Notre Dame.

"Only a coupla drinks to settle my nerves with the chest pains. Only one or two." He tried hard to be convincing as he wobbled around the living room in a circle several times, a ship without a rudder.

"What are you looking for? Shouldn't we hurry to the ER?" I asked sarcastically. I glanced over at the dismayed look on Dar's face and resisted the urge to laugh out loud. I did feel somewhat sorry for her; she meant well, but I'd been down this road too many times. The only way for her to understand would be to experience it for herself. He finally located the keys.

"OK. Let's go. Which hospital do you want to go to?"

"Hamot is the closest and they take my insurance." He should know, he'd been admitted there under the same pretense so many times that the staff should have sent him Christmas cards. They would run a battery of tests that lasted a week or so, which was his real reason for the charade. He would get time off from work, a wait staff and detox with meds, all compliments of insurance and the union. He'd gotten a union job after the divorce and loved it. He had pulled this trick at least twenty times, but management couldn't touch him and he knew it. He was "sick".

I opened the front door to Dar's car and motioned my father in. Dar raised her eyebrows at my uncharacteristic thoughtfulness toward him. As I closed the car door, I leaned over the top of the small Civic and bent toward the driver's side so that only she could hear me.

"I want to be in the back, out of range when he pukes," I whispered, then burst into cruel laughter at the dismayed look on her face. Poor Dar grew up in a nice family and was completely out of her league. She had no point of reference for our family's alcoholic drama. Dar set a land speed record getting to the hospital. She was as pissed as she was concerned and I couldn't fault her for it, but she couldn't say that I didn't warn her. She'd put herself in the position she was in and she knew it. I'd been down this road more times than I could count. People often thought that I was exaggerating about my parents until they experienced them personally, then they were pissed because they claimed that they hadn't been warned. As Sam used to say, "For those who understand, no explanation is necessary. For those who don't, no explanation is possible."

My father started gagging. He wheezed, "Pull over into this drug store," and pointed at the drug store coming up on the left. I knew what was coming. As Dar rolled into the parking lot, Wild Bill dug into his pocket and peeled a hundred dollar bill from a roll of them. I got out of the car as he waved it out of the front window. "Go in and get shom paper towelsh. I'm gonna be shick."

If I hadn't heard this so many times, I would have had a hard time figuring out what he was saying. I cut a wide berth away from him and the cash. I didn't want to chance getting too close and taking a direct hit. When I returned to the car with the paper towels, I saw that he had at least made it to the sidewalk and spared the Honda. I took the wrapper off of the towels and tossed the roll toward him before I got back into the car. This time, Dar didn't suggest that I go over and help him. We waited for him in silence as he wiped himself off. When we got to the hospital, Darla turned to pull into the guest parking lot.

"Where are you going?" I asked curtly. She looked at me as though I'd lost my mind.

"Into the hospital parking lot," she said very slowly. The "asshole" in that sentence was silent, but clear.

"No, you're not. Pull up over there, in front of the Emergency Room."

Dar looked relieved that I had seemingly located some sense of filial piety within myself. In actuality, I just knew the next page in this script and there wasn't an ounce of parental respect in it. She turned around and drove right up in front of the front door to the ER.

I jumped out and opened the car door for my father, who had nodded off. "Here we are." I grabbed his shirt sleeve and gave a tug to wake him up. He pulled himself out of the car and staggered to his feet. I walked him over to the automatic door of the ER and waited until it slid open. As he walked through the hospital doors, I turned around and jumped back into the front seat of the car that he had just vacated.

"OK, let's go! I need a drink!" I said cheerfully.

"What the fuck! Are you just going to leave him there?"

"Yup! This is far from his first roundup." I looked toward the door to see my father standing there uncertainly. I waved. To my surprise, he waved back and then turned and tottered through the doors. Mission accomplished.

CHAPTER TWELVE

1982

Still dressed in one of the standard pantsuits that I wore as an IBM Customer Engineer repairing mid-range computers, I stood in the narrow doorway of my Aunt Kay's tiny kitchen drinking Tanqueray and tonic and watching her hover over a large pan of clam sauce. Aunt Kay was my mother's older and only sibling and I loved her with as much fervor as I hated her sister. Although sisters, there were never two people further apart in appearance, temperament, or personality. It wouldn't be a stretch to consider that one had been switched at birth.

My aunt lived in a well-kept older home. Her three-story brick house was located in a quiet, middle-class neighborhood and her house immediately stood out each spring and summer, ablaze in colorful flowers adorning her tiny front yard. Tulips and daffodils vied for her attention in the spring. In the summer, flower boxes adorned every windowsill and the front of the small stoop. Each box was home to dozens of purple, blue, and pink pansies. The pansies seemed to have tiny faces that beamed, as delighted to be at her house as almost everyone who visited. Inside, the house furnishings leaned toward Victorian antique with just enough of a modern flair to ensure that a visitor wouldn't confuse it with a home belonging to someone's grandmother. A proud woman, Aunt Kay held herself and her home to a much higher standard than my mother did.

Aunt Kay was still dressed in her work clothes as well, but had traded her heels for white cotton mules with open backs. Always glamorous in an Elizabeth Taylor sort of way, she could have worn burlap and easily worked a runway. The only reason Richard Burton settled for Liz was because my aunt was far too busy flirting with every man that she came in contact with in our Pennsylvania hometown, and never made it any further west than Ohio. In addition to having movie star glamour, my aunt had a machine gun wit. She had an opinion on everything and a one-liner to go with it. Between her looks and her intelligence, she was irresistible – and not just to men. She had dozens of friends, many since high school. Aunt Kay was just one hell of a good time. Her wit got even better after a few drinks and no one could get enough of her, including me. My aunt was a receptionist at a local manufacturing facility, and visiting salesmen kept her in a steady supply of dates. She was often out dining, drinking, and dancing four or five nights a week, a practice that went on for years. I made it a point to visit at least once a week on her off evenings and it was a rare evening when I had to her to myself.

Due in no small measure to my aunt's influence, I had systematically given myself a complete makeover. Since I was now working for a large computer company, I was finally able to afford shopping at the nicer department stores in town. With the advice of their helpful saleswomen, I learned how to dress professionally. A size 6, I was easy to fit, but I required extensive guidance in style and color matching. Losing the Scout Finch coif, my hair was fashionably styled and the local Estee Lauder ladies helped as much with makeup as their colleagues had with color coordinating blouses. My transformation was so complete that classmates from high school didn't recognize me when I made office calls to service their company computers. I hadn't achieved the natural glamour of my aunt, but the witness protection program would have been proud. If only I could have found a friendly sales clerk to provide an internal makeover just as easily.

In addition to her Elizabethan impression and rapier wit, my mother's older sister was a gourmet cook, incapable of cooking for less than six people no matter how many actually sat down at the table. As my aunt fussed over the clam sauce and put water on to boil for accompanying linguine, we exchanged family gossip. In the background, a Clancy Brothers tape played. Her favorite Irish band sang their songs of England's tyranny and Celtic pride from the large cassette player in the dining room with removable speakers. Aunt Kay never laid eyes or ears on a piece of Ireland she didn't love. An Irishman was a double winner as far as she was concerned, and she married and divorced two of them. She loved them; she just didn't particularly care for living with them. A true gourmet, tasting here and tasting there, she never knew if a better flavor (or Irishman) lay just over the horizon. A charter member of the local Irish Cultural Society, my aunt seemed to imagine that she was a recent arrival from the Auld Sod and would be packing soon for her imminent return. Fortunately, the ICS ran more on intention than pedigree. If you could drink, lass, well then, you're one of our own and a warm welcome to ye.

I liked to play pretend as much as Aunt Kay did, but my imaginings ran a little closer to home. I liked to purport that my aunt was my real mother, and I floated in a fairy tale of normalcy when I was at her house, just another smiling pansy. I embraced her as my mother with all of the enthusiasm that she embraced the Irish as her own. Fortunately, she was as tolerant of my imaginings as the ICS was with hers. If life were fair, I really would have been my aunt's daughter. But I'd long ago quit expecting life to deal the cards without a few quick cuts to favor the house – life was the house, and the house never lost. I got zapped at birth with some bad cards and some shit karma. I drew the short straw; I was stuck with Gertie, the loser sister and the asshole she married. I wanted the winner sister. I wanted Elizabeth Taylor in *The Last Time I Saw Paris* and I got Bette Davis in *What Ever Happened to Baby Jane.*

The heat from the kitchen was a welcome respite from the winter drafts in the old house. In addition to the linguini and white clam sauce, Aunt Kay had prepared a Caesar salad and had fresh garlic rolls in the oven. The mountain of food was just for my aunt and I, and it would be difficult to claim that I wasn't hungry after watching her cook for the last couple of hours. She was as incapable of cooking without a drink in her hand as she was of cooking for less than an army, but booze put her in slow-mo. As the result, it took two or sometimes three times as long to turn out a meal as one would think, but there was no hurry. I was feeling the slow pull of Tanqueray magic myself. No hurry at all. Moving the clear cocktail glass in circles so that the sliver of lime swirled round in the gin and tonic, I was comforted by the sound of the ice in the glass. With my fourth cocktail on an empty stomach, the world's sharp edges had dulled and were decorated with a fuzzy mist, just the way I liked them. The smell of my aunt's special recipe linguini and clam sauce cooking on the gas stove was delightful enough to tempt the angels from their heaven. But I had a dilemma. I hated to eat while I was drinking. It put a real damper on the buzz. No matter, I decided. There was a half quart of gin left and two fresh bottles of tonic on the cold back porch. It would be more than enough to drown the negative effects of the meal on my warm, alcoholic glow.

"What do you think happened to my mother, Aunt Kay?" I asked.

A stranger in the room would have surmised that the topic had just come up out of the blue. But discussing my mother was our favorite conversation and we never tired of it, despite the fact that neither of us had seen my mother in years. Either of us could bring it up at any time, and there were endless labyrinthian paths that the ensuing discussion could take. Like all alcoholic discussions, it had no beginning, no end, and no exit.

For most of my life, I considered my mother evil incarnate. I struggled to even think of her as my mother. She demonstrated no kindness or caring toward her children, instead seemingly bent on drumming lessons into us with a measure of callousness that seemed to give her a great deal of pleasure. Even as a child, I understood that love is sometimes harsh. I learned from the aged encyclopedias that the first thing that a mother giraffe does to her newborn attempting to stand is to knock it down. Once it makes its way back to its feet, she knocks it back down with a gentle kick. Again and again she kicks its feet out from under it, until it is too exhausted to stand. The mother giraffe's apparent cruelty has a practical application; she understands too well that in order to survive predators, the first lesson her calf must learn is to get to its feet quickly.

However, my mother was no giraffe; her kicks were aimed to get her kicks. There was no predator outside the house that could be greater than those inside. Growing up, I could come to no other conclusion regarding her actions other than the fact that she was born evil. Concentration camp survivor and eminent psychiatrist Doctor Viktor Frankl observed that no matter what the circumstances, whether inside the confines of the camps or without, he found only two races of people to exist: those who were decent and those who were unprincipled. Although all humans are a mixture of good and evil and no one of us is one hundred percent one or the other, Doctor Frankl concluded that essentially one characteristic divides the two groups: the trait of kindness. According to Doctor Frankl, "Human kindness can be found in all groups, even those which as a whole it would be easy to condemn. The boundaries between groups overlapped and we must not try to simplify matters by saying that these men were angels and those were devils." In other words, not all guards are cruel and not all mothers are kind. Based on my mother's complete lack of kindness in any way, I could only conclude that she was essentially wicked. But evil is not inevitable. I have come to a gradual awareness that my mother wasn't born evil, she was broken. However, it would be difficult to pinpoint the exact event on the chart of her life where the break occurred.

"I wish I knew, honey." Aunt Kay stood at the stove, fixated on the boiling pot of linguine as though the contents couldn't progress to the desired tenderness without a witness. There was no greater sin in my aunt's book than overcooked pasta.

My aunt didn't know about my mother's Imp routine. I had pretty much forgotten the specifics by then myself, although the feelings were never far away. She knew I hated her sister, but who didn't by then? My mother and her increasingly bizarre behavior had inflicted so much damage and in such a wide circumference by that point, there was a very short list of people who could put up with her. So inseparable throughout their entire lives that they'd had special nicknames for each other, Aunt Kay and my mother were no longer speaking. Her sister was as tight-lipped as ever about whatever transgression had been committed and gave up no reason for the silent treatment. No one, including their mother, knew why. My mother hung up whenever her sister called and wouldn't answer the door when Aunt Kay went to her house. She had also recently taken to drunk-dialing my aunt's friends late into the night. This was long before caller ID and voicemail, so Aunt Kay's friends would answer the phone around midnight thinking that someone must have died for the phone to ring so late. They would be surprised to hear my mother's furious voice, raging vague diatribes about her sister: short on details, long on profanity. When it got to be too much, they gently hung up. None of it made any sense, but little about my mother ever did and the puzzle pieces that made up my mother's jigsaw were quickly disappearing into thin air.

Aunt Kay took a long drag from the Virginia Slims pursed between her Revlon lips as though coaxing some insight from it. She furrowed her perfect brow and peered at me through heavy mascara and tobacco exhaust as she exhaled, smoke mingling with the steam from the stove. In a voice slightly husky from years of tobacco therapy, she said, "I just don't know. Your mother was always a little, well...off. Not enough that anyone outside the family would notice, mind you. Just, *different.*" She coughed from the smoke. She'd been smoking for over thirty years at that point, and her lungs were beginning to protest. Clearing her throat, she continued.

"She was always like a child, despite my parents' efforts to make her grow up." She shook her head at the memories. "My mother, father, and I worked in their store, and it was your mother's job to keep up the house. She was paid well for it."

I listened intently, swirling my glass.

"One winter, the pots and pans gradually disappeared until there was almost nothing left in the house to cook with. It drove your grandparents nuts." After another quick drag, she pushed the smoke out through her nose. "Who in the hell would make off with some friggin' pots and pans?" she asked rhetorically. She went on, "When they asked your mother if she had a clue, she would shrug her shoulders and smile. Typical Gertie." Aunt Kay mimicked a goofy grin and shoulder shrug. "We couldn't figure out what the hell had happened until spring thaw. As the snow melted, we found the pans in the backyard. Instead of washing the pans after dinner, she had put them out in the snow and left them there!"

I shook my head in disbelief.

She continued, "She thought her little secret was hilarious until my father took the razor strap to her. It wasn't quite so funny then." The cigarette dangled from her mouth as she turned back toward the stove. Interrupting herself for moment to flick the ash into an ashtray already half full, she caught it just in time. Red lipstick surrounded the filter tip of every discarded butt. She returned the shrinking cigarette back to her lips; it dangled down as though held in place by a magnet. She squinted through the smoke. "I'll tell you what, though. She loved your father. Loved him." Another drag. Another voyage around the linguine pot for the spoon.

The pasta was finally reaching critical mass, so my aunt tabled the conversation for a few minutes and returned the cigarette to the crowded ashtray for good. She interrupted the process long enough to take a long swallow from her favorite drink, a large yellow plastic tumbler of Irish with just enough water to baptize it a cocktail. Aunt Kay was refined. A lady. She would never drink anything straight up. She nodded her head toward the cup. "Go ahead and fix me another, please. Make sure that you don't drown the Irish. I need to keep an eye on this. I hate it past al dente, it seems so insipid."

In addition to her Irish refill, a Penn Shore Vineyards Chardonnay would nicely accompany both the white clam sauce and my pleasant boozy haze. I poured the wine into the small antique goblets at the table, while my aunt raced against time to produce the perfect pasta. By the time she'd carefully assembled the seafood and linguine on each plate, I'd set the table and brought in the salad and rolls. She butted another cigarette's red ash into an empty ashtray in the dining room. She'd smoked it only halfway and it would be relit after dinner.

She took her seat at the head of the table and our favorite conversation continued. There was no telling which path she would go down. She said, "When your father was stationed in Germany, your mother wrote him long, long letters every day. She would sleep by the phone at night, waiting for him to call. Sometimes he would, sometimes he wouldn't." She shrugged a shoulder, implying that Wild Bill Frombach may have found more interesting prospects on those evenings that my mother had slept by a silent phone. She picked at the linguine with her fork, put it down and then changed her mind again, momentarily adrift in Irish and memories. She lifted a forkful of linguine with small chunks of clam and parsley to her fading red lips and thoughtfully chewed it. It was followed by the yellow tumbler. Putting her hand up to her head, she methodically pulled the ends of her perfectly coiffed jet-black hair through brightly polished nails, a long-standing habit indicating serious thought or anxiety. Waiting for a man to call, or anyone really, was beyond her power of comprehension. She had no point of reference. Aunt Kay had gone out with hundreds of men, while the number of men that my mother dated in her entire lifetime could easily be counted on one hand.

She continued as though I hadn't heard this story a hundred times, "He called her one night right after he was discharged. He had nowhere else to go and slept on his sister's couch for a few months, but he didn't have a pillow. Your mother walked nine miles in the bitter cold at one o'clock in the morning to bring him one from our house. She had such a good heart then."

The person who walked miles through the snow to bring someone a pillow wasn't the mother that I knew. The mother that I had wouldn't cross the street to benefit anyone except herself. I rolled my eyes and relieved the wine glass of most of its contents; conversations about my mother demanded alcohol by the gallon. I snorted. "Nuts. That's what she was. Nuts. Who in the hell would do something like that?" I never tired of any of the stories, although they never changed. "What else, Aunt Kay? What else?" I was looking for her to trip up one day and reveal the real deal. I hoped for a slip of the tongue after too much Irish that would indicate a secret compartment behind a story, just once. I was a detective in my mother's life, sifting through the testimony of a witness for inconsistencies; looking for that point on the chart. There. The break occurred right there. In the long run, my aunt didn't provide the

Rosetta Stone to my mother's psyche. It turned out that it was right under my nose the entire time, although it would take me many years to recognize it.

Our favorite conversation typically lasted into the night, tapering into a general swapping of family gossip. She asked about the rest of the family, but Aunt Kay always specifically inquired about Mary Pat, who had basically gone radio silent since she'd moved out of my mother's house as a high school sophomore. We were all concerned about her, but my aunt seemed to take her absence personally. She always said that she prayed for Mary in her nightly prayers. It turned out that she hadn't prayed quite hard enough.

CHAPTER THIRTEEN

1985

The effects of alcoholism and drug addiction are like a chemical boa constrictor: a slow but persistent serpent that takes its own sweet time to slowly suffocate its victim. However, there are other times when the disease loses patience and extends a bony arm from the grave to seize immediate gratification.

My little sister, Mary Pat, was struck down and killed as she crossed a dark, busy street in Erie at 1:15 a.m when she was twenty-three years old. After a night of drinking with a friend, she had gone into a bar to get a six-pack to finish up the night. Her undoubtedly less than sober friend waited in the car across the street. She was busily involved changing the radio station when the accident occurred and was completely unaware of what had happened. Her story changed twice in the police report.

According to the report, Mary was hit hard enough to knock her out of her shoes, projecting her body eighty-five feet. After landing in the opposing lane of traffic, she was then hit three more times. The police were unable to locate any of the vehicles, and no one was ever charged for the crime.

Subject: Hit & Run car/pedestrian accident #10-319
Investigation indicates the pedestrian was crossing Peach Street from east to west. Unit #1 was southbound and struck the pedestrian. Impact with the vehicle propelled the pedestrian southward. The victim was struck with force sufficient to be knocked from shoes. The victim was propelled thirty-five feet and

struck the road surface at one point and continued south another fifty feet before coming to rest in the northbound lane. Witness states that while the victim was lying in the street three different northbound cars hit the body. Unit #1 did not stop after hitting the pedestrian. None of the northbound vehicles stopped at the scene.

AUTOPSY

PROVISIONAL ANATOMIC DIAGNOSIS

Massive trauma
Extensive skull fractures with partial brain evisceration
Transected thoracic aorta with hemorrhagic dissection
Lacerated liver
Ruptured urinary bladder
Extensive soft tissue abrasions and lacerations
Multiple fractures of lower extremities
II. Additional diagnosis – Postmortem blood alcohol level (pulmonary artery) .140%

Witness Interview

Q. *I understand that you have some information about the above listed accident?*

A. *I was in my apartment when I heard the "thud" of something being hit. I ran to the window and saw something in the street. I also saw a mint-green car going fast south on Peach from the area. The car was midsized, like a Volvo or Benz. I ran down the stairs and to the street. I saw it was a person in the street and I turned to my wife and told her to call the police. She went back upstairs and I went in the street. I saw some cars coming north on Peach and I tried to flag them down for assistance. I saw they were coming very fast, I think they were drag racing, so I got out of the street. The person that was driving the car in the center lane had dark curly hair and it was a dark car. I saw the driver laughing at the car beside him; that is why I think they were drag racing. Also the fact that they were going very fast. The car in the center lane hit the person lying in the street. The passenger-side tires went over the* *mid-section of the person. This car was a full-size car like a Chevrolet. I don't know what make it was. There was another car following them. I tried to flag him down and he swerved toward the center of the road. His passenger-side tires ran over the legs. I thought he was going to stop because he slowed down, but then he kept going. I was on the curb again. I ran to my doorway. I didn't see the third car hit the person, but I heard it. I went to my door because my daughter was coming down the stairs and I didn't want her out there. I started to go back over to the person in the street and then people started to run out of the bar.*

If our family had been normal, we would have taken Mary's death as our wakeup call. It would have been the catalyst that finally brought us all together, like the activating agent in a kind of familial epoxy. If this were a movie, we would all stand together at the gravesite with a picture of Winona Ryder on the casket. We would wrap our arms around each other, finally united and grateful for the family we had left. But normal was an unfamiliar concept for us, and life isn't art. Instead of bonding us closer, Mary's death did just the opposite; it provided the sledgehammer that finished the job booze had started. The fragments of our family, already so broken from alcoholism, fractured completely like a cracked bottle that finally exploded into a million jagged pieces. We all reminded each other of things that were just as soon forgotten; as though we could hide our own psychic wounds and scars until we saw them in reflected in each other. That constant remembrance was far too painful for any of us to bear, so we banished each other from our respective lives.

My ice queen mother, usually so frigid and fierce, never again uttered Mary Pat's name without breaking down in tears. Wild Bill was so falling-down drunk at the viewing that we assigned less drunk family members rotating shifts prop him up. Beth and I managed the funeral and our parents, as we always managed everything. And, at the end of the day, we remained unforgiven for being the sisters that survived.

CHAPTER FOURTEEN

1986

As time went on, I excelled at work by day and drank myself blind every night. Although I passed out most nights with my face on the bathroom floor, I knew I wasn't an alcoholic. Alcoholics like my father puked their guts up every morning and since I wasn't a barfer, I wasn't like them. Although I wasn't a habitual Gennie drinker like my parents were, it had gotten to the point where I wouldn't turn one down. No one ever said a word to me about my alcohol consumption because no one thought a thing of it. I had a great job and seemed to be living a normal life. But there weren't a lot of people that I knew that had a "normal" measuring stick that they lived by. With the exception of my grandparents and Beth, almost all of my friends and relatives also drank themselves into oblivion on a regular basis. The drinking pattern that had so bothered me growing up was now the norm.

Aside from my drinking buddies, I remained a loner. I dated here and there, but couldn't maintain a relationship for any length of time. People just got in the way of drinking. Lovers came and went, but no one seemed to stick around. I still couldn't count on anyone or anything except the singular constant that my family had been leaning on for years – alcohol. But it was different with me, because I was different from all of them. I wasn't a beer drinker like my parents or a whiskey drinker like my grandfather. I was an uptown gin gal. High class. Refined. IBM employee. Gin was my best friend, my constant companion. Always right there, always right now. If my parents had found gin instead of Gennie, maybe they wouldn't be as fucked up as they were. I'd drink to that.

Finally, I maneuvered my way into a promotion to Boca Raton, FL. Boca was the home of the IBM Personal Computer Division, which was just getting off of the ground. The PC had been wildly successful beyond anyone's imagining and Boca needed bodies. My manager sent me south on a six-month temporary assignment with the farewell message that if I found a job, I could stay. A well-placed case of beer can get you far in this world, and it worked its magic for me again in this instance. A case of Iron City to a Pittsburgh native in a nearby office resulted in an interview and then a job. Goodbye, cold weather and crazy family. At long last, I was unshackled from my family and hometown for good. IBM not only moved me to Boca, but bought me a house to sweeten the deal. I had arrived.

Although I'd given my family the geographic slip, I brought my biggest problem with me: myself. As my drinking continued its progression, the personality changes came faster and got worse. With the first drink, I'd leave my IBM persona behind and turn into Party Girl, everyone's favorite. Sometime between the second and fifth drink, I got weary of Party Girl and the Real Me arrived, the Me that I'd inherited from generations of alcoholics and the one that I couldn't stand in my parents: Psycho-Bitch. My temper, usually only visible just below the surface, erupted like Mount St. Helens with flames and fangs. My ugly mood swings seemed to get uglier and last longer. At times I could barely stand myself. I often wished that I could drop myself off at the beach for the afternoon.

In addition to the alcoholic progression, the burden at work was enormous. My position as an IBM Service Planner was considered a management training position and my immediate supervisor considered it his personal mission to make the position a management boot camp. He, of course, filled the role as our personal drill instructor. Inspired by Hell Week for Navy SEALs, he considered it his personal mission to see what we were made of. Eighty-hour work weeks were not uncommon. I once made a set of charts projecting warranty returns and defects for a certain product which he promptly dismissed, sending me back to the drawing board. Two sleepless weeks and over three hundred charts later, I wearily presented him with the original charts, which he finally approved with a huge smile.

Shortly after getting settled at IBM Hanoi Hilton, I found out that Nova University offered a program to IBMers at the Boca plant who had some college credits and wanted to finish their degree. By attending classes every Thursday evening and every other Saturday, students could earn a B.S. in two and a half years. Pat was still nagging me on a regular basis about finishing my degree, and although my long-ago college dream had dimmed, it hadn't died. I had no idea where I would find the time, but I signed up anyway.

Since I could never have enough insanity in my life, I also started dating a woman who was putting herself through chiropractic school in Los Angeles by selling cocaine to her classmates. She was a nice enough person and I know that I liked her, but I liked the free coke even more. Like a true addict, I enjoyed any kind of high. But the best thing about cocaine was that it enabled me to drink a lot more and enjoy the buzz for a lot longer before I passed out. It never once occurred to me to stop drinking to enjoy the effects, I just needed a little chemical boost to make it last. When my friend graduated and quit dealing for a career as a licensed chiropractor, I ditched her. Since the free ride had ran out, I also stopped doing coke. That shit was expensive, and I could buy a lot of gin for what an eight ball cost on the street.

During our relationship, the chiropractor was the first to suggest therapy. "You're out of touch with your feelings," she said.

Friends soon jumped on the bandwagon. "You seem to be under a lot of pressure," they said. The only feelings I ever knew were anger and rage, and the world had pretty much had its fill of me getting in touch with those feelings. I'd been under pressure my whole life: thirty years by that point. I was on constant high alert for someone or something to attack me, and it took every ounce of energy that I had to pretend to be normal. That type of vigilance took its toll, and the cracks in my personality were just getting too wide to hide or ignore any longer. Typical of many functioning alcoholics, I could hold it together when I needed to, but became completely unhinged and over-reactive over the slightest situations.

I once went into an insane rage over spotting a stop sign at a location where I'd never seen one before. I wasn't pulled over, there were no police in sight. No one ran the red light or cut me off. There wasn't a damn thing going on. Nothing. Just a red sign with white letters, quietly doing what it does best. STOP. I pulled the car over and beat the steering wheel for a half hour or more, screaming my head off. I'm sure that I quite rightly terrified the person in the car with me. There was absolutely no logical reason for the meltdown. Perhaps I didn't care for that shade of red on that particular day. Or, maybe I considered it a message from the universe that there was a long list of things that I should really STOP doing. More likely, I just wanted life to STOP.

CHAPTER FIFTEEN

1987

I sat warily in the plaid chair. The office of the affable-looking woman sitting in the chair across from me was just as pleasant as she was. I'd picked her name out of the phone book.

"What made you pick up the phone?" Eileen asked. She gave me a friendly smile and her dark eyes twinkled behind black-framed glasses.

"I'm a chronic liar and I have no feelings."

Her friendly smile vaporized instantly, like air punched from a balloon. A slight vertical line flashed momentarily between manicured eyebrows, gone as quickly as it appeared. She recovered rapidly. But I could tell that the new smile was fake, a theatre mask. She asked, "Could you repeat that?"

She was playing for time, but I had no idea why.I replied, "I lie when it would be just as easy to tell the truth and I don't experience feelings as other people apparently do." I wanted to explain, hopefully banishing the faux face and bringing the real smile back. I wondered why she'd suddenly lost her cheeriness, but I wondered more why I cared one way or the other since this was the first time I'd ever met her. I'd never been to a therapist before and hoped that this wasn't her first roundup as well; one of us had to lead this dance. I leaned forward to get a closer look, as though assessing her combat readiness. She appeared to be in her early forties, at least old enough chronologically to have been around the block a few times. I tried to relax, reminding myself that I had picked her because she had the apex PhD after her name. But within my brain an internal trial ensued, the counsel for the prosecution arguing that book smart doesn't mean street smart.

If she could sense the heightened scrutiny, she ignored it, focusing on her notepad on which she furiously scribbled.

"Would you mind taking a few tests?" Eileen asked, not glancing up from her notes. "You don't have to, of course, but it would help me reach a diagnosis more quickly." I wasn't sure that I liked the word "diagnosis", but I immediately agreed, hoping that it would speed up the process and we could wrap this up in a couple of sessions. I had no intention of becoming a therapy junkie, a sitcom punch line unable to navigate the simplest decision without consulting my shrink. My intention was to get in and out before anyone found out that I was in therapy. I pictured the process as sort of a quick-change mental dressing room. If I couldn't rapidly grab some new feelings off the rack, I would at least learn to wrap my issues in a nice shawl to cover up the stains. Out came the ink blots and we began.

I took a number of psychological tests that day, filling out forms and naming black blobs for at least two hours. At the conclusion, Eileen told me that she'd review them and we would discuss the results at my next appointment the following week. I noticed that she avoided using the word "session". I also noticed that the fake smile had taken up residence. During the tests, I'd noticed that some of the questions were repetitive, although the wording could be somewhat different. During the week before my next "appointment", I convinced myself that I really enjoyed an unfair test-taking advantage. I am a pretty good test taker, as anyone would be who survived nuns and the Army. Many people aren't good at testing, and most probably wouldn't notice the pattern-like nature of the questions. Could that be considered cheating? Should I mention it to Eileen or just sit back and enjoy my secret weapon? The more I thought about it, the smugger I got. If those tests were the best that the psychology field had to offer, I probably didn't even need therapy! I almost couldn't wait for my appointment so that I could find out how high I'd scored.

I practically skipped into Eileen's office at the appointed time and immediately noted that the real smile was back in full bloom. Of course it was, I mentally congratulated myself. She had probably never seen such a high score and might even have already begun work on a magazine article for *Psychology Today*. I gave her a broad smile in return, anticipating my interview for the magazine.

"Well, good news!"

Sliding toward the edge of the sofa, I involuntarily held my breath as I awaited the documented verification of my brilliance. Too excited to speak, I nodded for her to continue.

"You're not a psychopath!" she announced happily.

I gaped. Was this some kind of joke? "Say what?"

"When you said that you were a chronic liar and had no feelings, I was initially concerned that you might be a psychopath. Those are the classic symptoms of psychopathy. Although more clinical terms are typically used, you essentially summed it up. But the test results demonstrate little tendency toward psychopathy!"

"Imagine my relief," I said dryly.

"Well, I was surprised because there are very few female psychopaths and those that are, rarely seek therapy."

"You could have just asked me."

"You said that you're a chronic liar. How would I know if you were telling the truth?"

Checkmate. Although I didn't know it at the time, that session was the beginning of the long road to recovery from the dark house of alcoholism and rage. I spent a year in therapy with Eileen, during which I started to be able to look at my childhood and began to admit that maybe it did indeed have some impact on my life. It was a small but significant step as, like many people, I wanted nothing more than to forget that the horror ever happened, to minimize it, to pretend that it was no big deal. Although she had initially misdiagnosed me as a psychopath, never once in that year did she ask if I thought that I was an alcoholic. Although she had that psychology PhD, I'm fairly certain that she had no idea that there are times when the line between the two is as slender at it is, and in some cases, blurred enough to be almost indistinguishable.

Many times when a person enters therapy or some other form of support and begins to change, it creates a backlash from their friends and family. People surrounding us have a vested interest in the status quo, as most of us have been doing the same things with the same people for years. If you've been bossing them around, they may not like it, but it keeps them from accepting responsibility for their own lives. If you have habitually let people walk all over you, they become accustomed to using your face as their doormat. When you start up the engine on your personal change-mobile, don't be surprised when you start finding tacks under the tires or the spark plug wires yanked. As we say in the corporate world, expect pushback. You can take that to the bank, so plan on it. I wish that someone would have given me that memo when I started changing. I wouldn't have stopped changing because I was so miserable...besides, it seemed as though once the process started, it took on a life of its own. But if I had known, it would have made it easier for me when they bolted. As it turned out, some people in my life liked to complain about my behavior, but it actually seemed that they were unhappy when I actually listened and the wheels of change began turning.

"How do you feel about that?" Eileen asked. The stock phrase of every therapist, this question is as essential to their profession as a scalpel to a surgeon. In essence, both are looking to accomplish similar goals, it's just that surgeons can actually see the blood during the operation. Both processes can be gory.

"I'm sorry, could you repeat that?" I had spaced out again, as often happened whenever I saw a feeling coming four blocks away. I'd been spacing out for years, the secret weapon that I'd developed so that my parent's abuse couldn't affect me. It had gotten worse since I started therapy. My friends called me a space cadet, but the official term is disassociation.

"How do you feel about the breakup of your relationship?"

"I'm fine with it." At the time, I considered myself pretty easygoing, although most people in my orbit would have vehemently disagreed with me. There were very few things that I thought I wasn't fine with. That is, until pesky things like stop signs popped up where

I didn't expect them. No one knew when those explosions would occur, including me.

"Do you love her?"

"I don't know what that means."

"You don't know what love means? Well, how do you feel about your mother?"

"I hate her. I hate her fucking guts," I said vehemently. Eileen had touched on one of the few things that I happened to be not fine with. No, not fine at all.

"How do you know that you hate her?"

"I know because I know."

"So you know what hate is because you know, but you don't know what love means."

"I never thought of it that way. But when you put it like that, it would seem that you're correct, although it is quite illogical," I said, going all Spock on her in self-defense.

"Do you love anything? Everyone loves something, even if it's only meatballs."

"I can't think of a thing, including meatballs," I said. It was true. By that point, I had no point of reference for love. I had become estranged from Beth and Aunt Kay and rarely spoke to Sam and Pat. I only had room in my life for drinking and could only identify one feeling: anger. It was the only emotion that made me feel alive inside. I was either angry or numb – the needle went left or right, nothing in between. It occurred to me years later that there actually was one thing that I loved at that time. If Eileen had just substituted gin for meatballs, I would have been able to tell her that I understood love.

The girlfriend originally left because I was an alcoholic psycho and then came back when she learned that I had started therapy. But she left again for good when I stopped lying to her. She had gotten accustomed to my lying, as does everyone who is involved with an alcoholic. I was like the punchline to the old joke – how can you tell if an alcoholic is lying? Their mouth is moving. Alcoholics have to lie, because we're lying to ourselves. We lie to ourselves about how much we're going to drink and then we lie to you about how much we drank. We swear that this time, we'll just have one – an impossibility.

We then tell ourselves the same lie about the next drink, and the next, and the one after that. If you (or the police) ask how much we've had to drink, we'll inevitably snap that we've only had a couple. We lie about what where we've been, what we've done, and who we've done it with. When we can't get away with an outright lie, we'll tell part of the truth, just enough to straddle the line between true and false. If pushed, we'll win on a technicality, because we've become damn good at the dark art of bullshit. But as time goes on, we get so good at lying that we can't tell what the truth is anymore, even to ourselves. Nor, at that point, do we care.

It got to the point where I lied when it would be just as easy to tell the truth. The girlfriend once asked idly if I'd gotten the chance to take my clothes to the dry cleaners. I said yes, knowing full well that they were still in the trunk of the car. It made absolutely no sense. The dry cleaning consisted of my work clothes, whether they went to the cleaners or not affected no one but me. Several hours later, when we went to put groceries in my trunk, there was the pile of skirts and blouses, obviously not at the cleaners.

"Why did you say that you'd taken your clothes to the cleaners?" She wasn't angry, just puzzled, as anyone would be.

I slammed the trunk. I didn't even have the grace to be embarrassed. "I don't know. Who the hell cares? You're always on my back." I came back at her with a vengeance to deflect my own confusion. People in my life were accustomed to my lying disguised as ambivalence. When asking what I wanted for dinner, they were accustomed to hearing, "I don't care." When they wanted to know what movie I wanted to see, they were used to my getting dead drunk and passing out in whatever movie was picked out, instead of just saying no.

As the result of growing up in alcoholic household where disagreement or speaking up could have disastrous consequences, I'd been outwardly compliant my entire life while continuing to do what I damn well pleased. The first step in leaving the Dark House meant the beginning of honesty, although I couldn't have told you that at the time. When I began changing, I had to begin telling the truth, albeit in fits and starts. I had to start small, because the concept was so foreign. I started indicating that I had a preference for dinner. I'd speak up when I really didn't want to go to the movies. Actually, it was more to the effect of, "No, I don't want to go to the fucking movies!" Being honest doesn't necessarily imply kindness or tact; at least, not at the beginning. Like learning any new skill, it was awkward at first. Telling the truth then was a feat in and of itself; it wouldn't get pretty for a long time.

Like many people in my life, the girlfriend was used to my compliance. When we got together, I had no opinion on anything. When I started speaking up, I changed the deal. One could say that I broke the deal.

"You have something to say about everything these days. I almost liked you better before therapy," she snapped several times.

"You're the one who came running when you heard that I was in therapy," I snapped right back.

She was gone shortly after that, the collateral damage of my personal growth. She was the first, but certainly not the last. Pushback. Expect it. Shaking up your status quo isn't for the faint of heart. Here's the good news, though: The payoffs are massive, almost on the scale of winning the lottery but far better: no taxman and scammers on your trail.

CHAPTER SIXTEEN

1987

After being in therapy for about a year and following *most* of my therapist's suggestions, life had calmed down and was actually going really well. The ugly mood swings seemed to have evened out, the college degree was within reach, and I'd even managed to stay out of a relationship for almost six months. I was still drinking, of course. But as far as I was concerned, I'd cut way back. Cutting way back meant "only" three or four drinks after work, but at least I'd stop when I had that pleasant buzz and long before my face hit the bathroom floor. People were even starting to compliment me on the changes in my behavior that therapy had helped me achieve. In essence, therapy had helped me get to where I'd always wanted to be: I was finally happy, or at least no longer wildly unhappy. Life was good!

When I'd first started working with her, Eileen had noted that she hadn't had much experience with or exposure to gay people, so I was a little bit of a novelty to her. As I wasn't struggling with my identity at the time and she was helping me to make progress in breaking through the ice flow that passed for my feelings, I didn't care one way or the other, as long as she wasn't homophobic. So I was surprised one day when she mentioning that she had another gay client.

"I'm wondering if you can help her," she asked.

I was stunned. How could I help one of her clients? I'd come a long way in the last year, but it was still a stretch by anyone's measure that I was helping myself on most days.

She continued on as though she had read my mind. "She's been married for ten years. She is divorcing her husband and is "coming out", as I think it's called. She works at IBM as well and doesn't have any gay friends. Perhaps she can network with you."

"Um, ok. I'm not exactly a gay paragon but I'll do what I can to help." Fort Lauderdale has been a gay mecca for years, but Boca Raton is twenty miles and a huge lifestyle change away from the gay mecca of Fort Lauderdale. My few gay friends in Boca were pretty closeted and I was too busy with work to make it to the gay bars down there very often. I told myself that I could at least tell her where the bars were, if nothing else.

I met her client, Margie, for lunch a few weeks later. She was attractive in a conservative upper-middle-class sort of way, resembling a pale, blondish Jackie Kennedy who had misplaced her pillbox hat. As we sat in the small Thai restaurant close to the IBM building where she worked, I listened to her story. I was impressed because although she had a lot going on, in true Jackie fashion she wasn't seeking sympathy nor whining about her complicated situation. She matter-of-factly related how her life had turned into the perfect storm. In addition to her soon-to-be ex-husband, she also had two children. Her husband had developed multiple sclerosis several years prior and was confined to a wheelchair. Angry at the shitty hand that life had unexpectedly dealt him, he had become abusive. He seemed to particularly pick on five year old Kerry, probably because she was the least able to defend herself. Hunt and attack the weakest gazelle, that's how bullies and predators roll. The most recent incident occurred when he chased Kerry around the house with his motorized wheelchair, using it to push the dining table and pin the little girl between the table and the kitchen wall. The incident was so severe that Margie had been forced to call 911 on him. She was terrified for herself and the children, so she had kicked her husband out of the house and initiated divorce proceedings.

Margie's matter-of-fact façade cracked somewhat when she discussed her seven year old son, Jerry. Quite naturally, he was upset over the changing family dynamics and had begun to act out. He demanded nonstop attention and didn't care where or who it came from, or how he got it. He mouthed off to everyone. No one was safe from his developing aggression, including strangers. As we ate Pad Thai, she related an event that had recently occurred during a visit to her parent's condo.

"I was sitting in the kitchen chatting with my parents and the kids were playing on the patio that overlooked the golf course. All of a sudden, I heard Jerry yelling at the top of his lungs. I couldn't make out everything he said. All I heard was the tail end."

"What did he say?" I couldn't imagine what a seven year old could shout that would be so upsetting.

"...and she wants to suck you off!"

"Holy crap! What was that all about? What did you do?"

"There was a couple playing golf and Jerry was yelling at them," she explained. "There wasn't much I could do by that point. I brought him inside the apartment and closed the door. I know he's upset about the divorce, but I don't know what to do and I don't want to upset him any further."

She told me that her strategy was to ignore his outbursts, hoping that they would soon be over. I would discover that Jerry knew that his mother gave him a long leash before he suffered any real ramifications for his behavior. He was an extremely bright child and had quickly learned that he'd become the boss of the house in his father's absence, so he took that freedom and ran with it. He constantly tested his mother's limits, delighting in his newfound freedom and power. Who wouldn't?

If all of that weren't enough of a recipe for a domestic disaster, Margie had also made the decision to come out as a lesbian. Neither Jerry Springer nor reality shows existed at the time, which was unfortunate, as there was already enough material in Margie's life for at least one show-out-the-cuckoo kind of episode. Soon enough, there would be enough drama to sustain an entire season for Mr. Springer.

As it turned out, in spite of her family situation, Margie and I had some things in common. In addition to working at IBM, we both enjoyed wine and reading, in that order. We also lived within walking distance of each other in West Boca Raton. We took to dropping by each other's house on weekends for a glass of wine or to swap books, and soon became involved. In hindsight, we both should have run the other way. At the very least, I should have just remained friends with her, letting her work out her numerous issues on her own before getting involved. But hindsight is 20-20. However, it doesn't *always* yield insight: look what it did for Lot's wife.

Although it seemed at the time that we shared a lot of interests, you could have counted the things we had in common on one hand. In retrospect, our relationship could have been summed up by Jennifer Coolidge's immortal improv line from the movie *Best in Show*: "We have so much in common, we both love soup and snow peas, we love the outdoors, and talking and not talking. We could not talk or talk forever and still find things to not talk about."

If we had talked a little more and drank a lot less, one or both of us may have experienced a moment of clarity. But the intensity of Margie's family drama drew me like a baggie to an addict. Children of chaos, active alcoholics can no more turn away from drama than we can from an open bar at a wedding. We're drama junkies. I was convinced that Margie just needed a good, strong pillar of strength who had survived family dysfunction and knew how to traverse those stormy seas. Little did I know that the gentle breeze that therapy had brought to my life for the past year was rapidly building a head of steam under the radar, the harbinger of an ass-kicking Category 5 hurricane. A storm of epic proportions was brewing, one that would make the stormy seas of my dysfunctional childhood seem like a smooth pond.

Since I'd found a relationship, I was convinced that I was cured and no longer needed therapy, so I parted ways with Eileen. She wasn't particularly thrilled with the way that her gay networking experiment had turned out, but wished me luck. I almost thought that I heard her murmur, "You'll need it," under her breath.

Although she'd moved her husband out of the house to be cared for by his sister, Margie's bitter divorce was far from finalized. Her ex-husband and his family picked a battle at every turn, hoping for a lucrative attachment to her IBM salary and future retirement. The last thing that she needed was to provide them with the ammunition that she had a lesbian lover. In addition, Margie lived in a close-knit, upper-class neighborhood where everyone waved at each other, hosted barbeques and pool parties, celebrated their kid's birthdays, and knew everyone else's business. If her neighbors had uncovered our affair, they would have happily let her ex-husband in on the news and then sat back to watch the fireworks.

To avoid a legal shitstorm, we met secretly for a year or so. After her kids were asleep, I'd park across the street from her development and tiptoe through the neighbors' yards to her back door. To say that I was less than thrilled with that arrangement is an understatement. I was a professional who owned my own home and was finishing my degree...and here I was sneaking through back yards like a thief in the night. But I was also aware that no one had a gun to my head. I knew it was my choice. So, despite my resentment and knowing that I was a complete idiot, I continued my midnight treks.

Sometimes I would meet Margie and the kids for pizza so that I could get to know them. The kids were adorable and intelligent. Jerry was a freckle-faced towhead who favored crew cuts. Kerry had a shy smile and it was obvious that she would grow up to be the spitting image of her mother. However, I was dismayed to find that I really hadn't realized how extreme Margie's habit of ignoring Jerry's outbursts was. She increasingly took direction from him to maintain the fragile family peace. As she didn't want to upset him any further than he already was over the divorce, she placated him with power, allowing him to make many decisions that affected our plans. He typically chose the family activities, restaurants, and timeframes. When he didn't get his way, he threw tantrums of epic proportions, ruining many family meals, just like my father had.

To me, it seemed as though time had rolled backward and a mini-me cast from my father's mold had materialized at my dinner table. After all these years, I still was still under the reign of a tyrant, but this one didn't drink and wasn't even old enough for an allowance. With all of the other balls that Margie had in the air, she was so tired from everything that she had no energy left to do battle with her strong-willed son. It was easier for her to just give in to him. But the more she acquiesced to his demands, the broader the demands became. I found myself in a recreation of my parents' house, with a vacuum of parental leadership. So, I did what I'd always done: I stepped up to the plate. Actually, as an adult, I staggered up to the plate and tried to grab the bat away from the kid. The family didn't have a prayer; a drunk in a power play with a child over family leadership. We all lost.

Marge was initially relieved that I wanted to participate in the family. As the divorce approached and we got closer to moving in together, she welcomed my willingness to join in parenting activities. She thought that she'd found a parenting partner. Unfortunately, the only parenting examples that I had were the ones demonstrated by my own massively dysfunctional relatives, who were surely heavily influenced by the Inquisition. I felt like an amateur painter who had only been influenced by the works of Picasso on a bad acid trip. Nothing good would come of it and the results could only be frightening. To my horror, and certainly to that of Margie and her kids, I rapidly became my parents incarnate. I was astounded to find myself saying the exact same things to those children that my parents had said to me. I acted exactly like my parents without the violence: constantly on the hunt for situations to criticize, over-punishing for minor transgressions, falling into fits of screaming rage at the slightest provocation (of which there were many). I would show Margie what real acting out was all about. If that act worked with her kid, I could top that in spades. I was a pro and had been doing it for years. Any modicum of self-control and calm that I'd acquired during the year in therapy vanished.

It was like watching a movie inside my own head: a horror film featuring a monster that will pop out of nowhere at any moment. I never knew when my monster would appear. Part of me knew that I was acting like my parents and had become a total nut job. But that part of me was completely powerless – it seemed as though it could only watch. I had the awareness that I was an asshole and appalled even myself, yet never once even attempted to control my own behavior. I never once had a cold moment of sanity and pulled the reins on myself, stopping before I went over edge of the abyss. Once the fuse was lit, I was as compelled to be an asshole as I was to continue drinking once I had that first drink. In rare moments of quiet, I would reflect on it. But my reflections were always immediately overwhelmed by anger, self-pity, and finger pointing. "They did this" and "they did that". Everything was their fault. I accepted zero responsibility. Not many drinking alcoholics do. It is ALWAYS us against the world, and the world never wins.

My drinking escalated dramatically because of the stress and so did Margie's. Yet, it didn't once occur to either one of us to get off the crazy train. Neither of us considered that moving in together wasn't a stellar idea under the circumstances. Well, under *any* circumstances. On our short list of things that we had in common, there was one conspicuous line item missing: children. Oh, we both loved them, all right. It's just that one of us loved the kids while they were awake and the other loved them a lot more when they were fast asleep.

Instead of leaving therapy, we should have rushed back to it, as we certainly needed professional help. But on the contrary, neither of us had any reservations about our decision to move in. Not a one. In fact, we actually couldn't wait to move in together! In retrospect, it was like sitting on death row and looking forward to the execution. Our decision was probably made in a similar environment as those made by death row inmates earlier in their careers – under the influence of massive amounts of alcohol. The moving van backed into the garage as the ink was drying on Margie's divorce papers.

The next couple of years went by in a blur as we slowly descended into alcoholic hell. My lifelong simmering rage had escalated to a fever pitch within the few years that I spent with Margie and her children; I was constantly one second away from reaching my boiling point. It was a boil that continually required a vent, a vent that could only be provided (and exacerbated) by alcohol. In my drunken musings, it often occurred to me that it was an interesting paradox that the substance that caused all of the problems was the only thing that made the problems bearable.

My verbal and emotional abuse escalated with my drinking. I was livid that I was stuck parenting children who had everything that I never had: a nice house and a mother who adored them, spent time with them, and provided almost everything they wanted. It was almost more than I could bear. I was drinking vodka straight by now, only using mixers in front of company. The additional booze accelerated my personality changes. By then, the original party girl in me that alcohol had brought out, the funny one, my personal Dr. Jekyll, was a hazy memory, leaving only Ms. Hyde on most days. Hyde was never far below the surface and sobriety didn't guarantee her absence, but the first drink guaranteed her immediate presence.

The small part of me that was appalled at this entire mess finally took action. I began to realize that I needed help to break the cycle of insanity that I was repeating, so I looked to therapy again. This time, I sought a therapist who specialized in alcoholic family issues, although I wasn't ready to quit drinking myself. Margie made it clear that she was relieved that I was doing the right thing by seeking therapy. She also made it clear that I was the designated patient. Since I was the one with the problem, I would be the one looking for a solution. I could count her out of the therapy equation. So I found a therapist that specialized in alcoholic families and began tinkering with the plumbing in my psyche again.

CHAPTER SEVENTEEN

1989

The late 80s ushered in a global recession and subsequent corporate layoffs that would permanently affect the way that corporations treat their employees. Previously impervious to recessions and even the Great Depression, IBM could no longer ignore the demands of the new Wall Street that howled for quarterly results and the subsequent stock punishment when those results weren't delivered. The computer giant provided the first and last generous severance package in its history, dangling an enormous sum like a carrot in front of thousands of regular employees like me in order to shrink payroll. In the days before "resource actions" and other corporate euphemisms for layoffs became commonplace, the tech leader offered two years' salary to leave the company. I jumped at the chance. After fifteen years of going to school part-time, I'd finally gotten the degree that meant so much to me. Years of taking business classes to acquire a B.S. in Business Administration had convinced me that I had the chops to become an entrepreneurial success. All I needed was some startup cash. IBM granted my wish: they cut me a six-figure check and set me adrift.

For most of my adult life, IBM had been my identity. They made me *somebody* after a childhood of being nobody. At party conversations when people asked what I did, I'd proudly announce that I worked for IBM. 'Nuff said. No one ever asked what my position was within the company. No need. It wasn't as though I was a powerful executive. I was a lowly engineer, a small cog in an enormous technical wheel. But the initials stood on their own. Being an IBMer gave me instant street cred in all areas of my life. No one questioned my drinking and there was little mention of my erratic behavior. Because of my job, some members of my family even grudgingly accepted my being gay. No matter what else I did or didn't do, I worked for IBM. How bad could I be? I even believed it myself.

Walking back to my car after depositing the large severance check, I unexpectedly broke into tears in the hot parking lot of the credit union. With my hands over my face, I stood stock still in the afternoon South Florida heat, sobbing uncontrollably – and I wasn't even drunk yet. Forcing my hands away from my face, I opened my purse and pretended to search for something as I walked back to the car to give myself time to pull it together. It wouldn't do to have a former co-worker pull up and see me in tears. The breakdown stunned me. For one thing, I never, ever allowed myself to cry: it was a futile sign of weakness that I'd abandoned to deprive my mother of the satisfaction of seeing me break. For another, I'd expected to feel elation after quitting, but instead I felt oddly rudderless. I now had a lot of money, but had sold my identity in the exchange. For the first time in my life, I felt something close to regret. I'd really wanted to leave IBM, but until that moment, I hadn't understood how much of my existence was invested in my career. I had just dynamited the bridge to corporate safety behind me and there was no way back over the abyss. I had prayed in a moment of weakness to leave the company, the first prayers that I'd uttered in decades. I could have said that my prayers had been answered. But in that moment, I wished that they hadn't been. As Saint Teresa of Avila reminds us, "There are more tears shed over answered prayers than over unanswered prayers." There was no way back and no clear path ahead. I was scared shitless. So scared that, in spite of myself, I started to pray again. I wasn't sure what to believe. I had stopped praying sometime during my childhood. I'd prayed for God to stop the Imp, but God never seemed to pick up the phone back then. I started dialing again in the parking lot.

They say that God never closes one door without opening another, but the time in the hallway between doors rarely feels spiritual. We're almost always in crisis at that point, making the wait seem interminable. I needed a door, any door. There was a boogeyman in the hall. It was too dark to see him, but I could surely feel his hot, evil breath. Unfortunately, I've never seen God rush that door-opening process, no matter what the crisis. Always taking His own sweet time, He never seems to show up until the instant before the boogeyman grabs us. I was to spend awhile cooling my heels in the hallway. But if there weren't hallways and we just went banging from door to door, would we ever really call for God?

I made my escape to the car without encountering anyone familiar and slowly slid into my new Mazda 929 sedan; a gift to myself while I still had a job that could secure a loan. As I sat numbly on the leather seat that still emitted that new-car smell, I caught my own eye in the rearview mirror. "Now who am I?" I asked my reflection. Silence echoed back from the abyss. It would get worse. There is nothing more yawn-inducing than the statement, "I used to work for IBM" (or anything else that someone *used* to do). We're only as good as our current gig, which explains why Cher keeps coming back.

Although I'd lost sight of it for that moment, I'd really left IBM for a reason. I knew *exactly* what I wanted to do: I was out for revenge. There were several events that fueled my fury: the death of Mary Pat, followed soon after by the deaths of my grandmother and Beth's husband from cancer. Our family had been repeatedly fleeced by a local funeral director. Like most undertakers, he had taken sales classes in manipulation that would have made a used car salesman blush. He upsold all the bells and whistles to grief-stricken people who could ill afford it. I wanted to get back at the funeral industry, so I opened a retail casket store.

Prior to 1984, funeral directors had a monopoly on all funeral consumables, including caskets. However, that year Congress (in a rare move benefitting the consumer) passed the federal Funeral Rule, which specifically states that funeral directors must use any casket provided by the customer for a memorial service. Although the law enabled anyone with a retail license to sell caskets, finding inventory was no easy matter. Today, you can buy a casket from Walmart or a host of other businesses. But at the time, all casket manufacturers and the funeral industry were engaged in an unholy alliance, and there wasn't a single casket company that would sell outside of the industry. I finally found a casket broker in California and bought twenty of them in various materials and styles. Locating the ideal retail space was important for the endeavor as it had to be large and visible, but not in a busy mall that would startle passersby. I found the perfect location in a strip mall that faced I-95 in Pompano Beach, just north of Fort Lauderdale. The showroom was in mint condition and there was a warehouse in the back to store excess inventory. The landlord assured me that if the business didn't work out, he wouldn't hold me to the five year lease. The Sterling Casket Company was open for business!

Owning a casket store leaves a person with a lot of time on their hands, time that I occupied getting drunk. Margie was becoming increasingly critical of my drinking. We both drank a lot, but she could stop for some period of time, whereas I wouldn't and then couldn't. To appease her, I told her that I stopped when she stopped. In reality, I just stopped drinking when she was around. I drank in the morning on the way to the casket store, stopping at different liquor stores to buy the small airplane bottles of booze. The tiny bottles offered several advantages: they could be quickly consumed and discarded, and they were also easy to hide. My favorite hidey hole was in the wheel well of my car. I polished off three or four of the small bottles by the time that I got to the store, passed out for a few hours in the warehouse and drank the rest for lunch. By the time I went home at night, I was more sober than not.

The therapist that I was working with had convinced me to join a group that she facilitated made up of women with similar family issues to my own. Most of those women were in recovery from drug and alcohol abuse and I finally started to take a look at my own dependence on alcohol. I was rarely stone cold sober any more, even when driving. I didn't care if I killed myself, as I'd wanted to die ever since I could remember. But I was terrified that I would hit someone, like my sister had been hit. I was even more terrified that I wouldn't know whether I had or not, and I checked the car every morning for signs of trauma, evidence that I may have hit someone in a blackout. I walked around it every morning without fail and examined it for damage – right before I got into the car and drove to the liquor store.

I knew that my daily game of alcohol roulette was a dangerous one on many levels and made up my mind to quit before it was too late. I still didn't apply the label of alcoholic to my own forehead. There were a lot of people in line for that tag before me. The big "A" belonged to my parents, and I was nothing like them. My problem was just that I had gotten into a bad habit of drinking all day. That habit definitely had to go, I just had to make up my mind to do it. I'd quit the bad habit of smoking, so I could cut back on the bad habit of drinking. I decided that I wouldn't drink for thirty days. I'd heard that new habits are developed after twenty-one days, so I gave myself an extra week to ensure that it took. Once it was no longer a habit, I could go right back to it.

I managed to quit drinking for almost three weeks. If I were a nut job with alcohol in my system, I was twice as crazy without it. Without the numbing sedative of booze, every resentment that I ever had came shrieking out of the woodwork. I blamed it all on Margie and the kids. They were to blame for everything that had gone wrong in my life. Family dinners began to resemble the shouting match meals of my childhood, only this time, I was in the starring role. I didn't throw any plates against the wall, but it wasn't because the thought didn't cross my mind. In the back of my mind, I knew that Margie wouldn't take as much as shit as my mother had. Margie had an invisible line in the sand and I intuitively knew that if it were crossed, the cops would be called. One night, Margie surprised me and came home with a bottle of wine.

"Would you like a glass of wine with dinner?" she asked casually.

I feigned a casual air as well, but my eyes were locked on that bottle from across the room like a Pershing missile on target. She had just offered me a free pass out of hell. "Sure. That would be nice," I said, just as offhandedly.

It was the first decent exchange that we'd had in weeks. After that, I gave up all pretense of control over alcohol and the next several months were one long continuous drunk fest. Margie took a family video that Christmas morning and in it, I looked like something that had crawled out of the crypt. Alcohol had added at least fifteen pounds of bloat, and it looked like every bit of it was in my face. My hair resembled that of a scarecrow, identical to my mother's when she was trashed. But the eyes were the worst: completely dead. I had the eyes of the psychopath that Eileen had original taken me for. Even though I was drunk again when we watched the video later in the day, I wasn't too drunk to finally recognize my nearly total physical transformation into my parents. My blood ran cold. I looked twice as bad as they had on their worst day. When in the hell had that happened? I made up my mind yet again. This was it. My New Year's resolution would be to put the booze down. Yet again, though, I was incapable of obeying myself. I couldn't even make it until noon on that New Year's Day, my birthday. The succubus alcoholism cackled in my face and I tossed back another shot so I couldn't hear her shrieks of laughter.

A couple of months later, Margie had finally taken all of the shit that she was going to, and she threw me out of the house. When she was packing up my things, she found dozens of empty mini booze bottles – in my shoes, pockets, drawers, behind books, anywhere there were a few spare inches. Since I had nowhere to go, I lived in the casket store warehouse with dozens of empty caskets. The metaphor wasn't lost on me. I also knew that the arrangement couldn't last long as I was not only broke, but in debt up to my ass. It had only taken a year to completely blow through my savings and IBM severance check. Although not as expensive as her cousins, cocaine and crack, booze is a demanding mistress. All addictions are pricey, but money is the least of the cost. Margie called me at the store shortly after I was kicked out.

"What the hell is wrong with you?" she shrilled.

"What the hell are you talking about?" I came right back at her. Although I was irritated with her for screaming at me, I was honestly puzzled. Had I called when I was in a blackout?

"Where the fuck did all of these bottles come from? Did you actually DRINK all of this?"

"What the hell are you talking about?" I repeated, although I now knew exactly what she was referring to. Although I was busted, the go-to alcoholic defense is denial, even to ourselves. Deny. Deny. Deny.

"There is something seriously wrong with you. You're a fucking alcoholic. Just like your fucking parents. Get the rest of your shit out of here tomorrow. You have between noon and five. If you're still here at five when I get back, I'm calling the police." She slammed the phone down.

With no Margie around, I didn't have to bother with those damn tiny bottles. After she hung up on me, I needed a drink. Fuck her. She and her normal little family had no idea what alcoholism was. I went to the liquor store down the street and got a quart of vodka, the favorite beverage of the hardcore alcoholic. We somehow think that the smell of vodka is inconspicuous; a premise as flawed as believing that dog pee isn't detectable because it isn't as bad as cat pee. As I sat at my desk in the store, drinking vodka out of a Dixie cup and looking at all of the caskets, I wondered again how to kill myself. I was broke. I was going to be homeless any day. I wanted to die, but I didn't want it to be painful. I wanted to end the pain, not suffer any more of it, physical or emotional. I had a gun, but couldn't get past visions of my aim being off just a hair and living a life as a vegetable, just conscious enough to know what I had done to myself.

I'd downed half of the quart and felt sick. I vaguely wondered what I could throw up as I had no idea when I last ate. Food can be a real buzzkill; you want an empty stomach so that you can rapidly get the full payload of the booze. It didn't occur to me at the time that non-alcoholics don't think of things that way. I don't remember getting to the bathroom in the warehouse, but evidently made it, as I came to with my face on the bathroom floor once again. It was pitch black, but I knew where I was because my shoulder was against the toilet. A familiar place and familiar position. The warehouse had been there for a long time. Over the years, who knew how many men had dribbled on the exact spot where my face met the floor. The prospect always occurred to me when I woke up there, but over time, it had ceased grossing me out. I didn't care enough to be repulsed any more.

More immediately, I didn't detect the telltale odor of vomit, so I was relieved that there would be no mess to clean up. I didn't think it was odd in the least that I could gather all of that information without vision and without moving a muscle. I reached out and my hand found the bottle. I would need it to dull the point of the hangover ice pick behind my temples. Fuck the Dixie cup – I downed the rest of the quart straight from the bottle. In the dark, there was no need for such formality between the bottle and me. Our intimacy went far beyond that. The vodka quickly kicked in, doing its job. The ice pick pain dialed back a bit so that the bite was bearable. But even a half quart of straight alcohol on a stomach that had a nodding acquaintanceship with food wasn't sufficient to get drunk enough to turn off my brain that night. Like everything else in my life, booze had failed me. It didn't keep its end of our bargain to stay forever and keep the world far enough at bay so that I could cope with the pain of living. As I lay in the un-air-conditioned, pitch black bathroom, propped up against the wall with the empty vodka bottle on the floor beside me, I experienced true alcoholic hell: too sober to be drunk and too drunk to be sober. I wondered for the umpteenth time since Margie had evicted me: How did it all come to this? I was doing so well. How could I have screwed up so badly?

Then, out of nowhere, I suddenly remembered something that I had heard one of my therapy pals once say that convinced her that she was an alcoholic. "I realized that I was powerless over alcohol and that my life was a train wreck as the result."

The thought went through my head like a lightning bolt. For some reason, it finally clicked when it never had before. If I had been more sober, I would have been electrified. What the hell? Could that really be it? Was it really the gin that had trashed my life? MY gin? My best friend? Could I really be an alcoholic? Even in my alcoholic netherworld state, I knew in my heart that the answer was yes. Not just yes. Hell, yes. Fuck, yes. Fuck me, I am just like them. I was only thirty-five, my parents had been drinking easily that long, twenty years longer than I had and even they weren't staring homelessness in the face. Not only was I just like them, I was even worse. They had been on a slow descent into hell for years. I was not only an alcoholic, I was a drunk on the fast track. Although half their age, I had somehow bypassed them on the road to imminent alcoholic destruction. Hi there, Captain Howdy, man. I didn't expect you so soon.

CHAPTER EIGHTEEN

1990

I had made up my mind to stop drinking numerous times, and had managed to do so only once. The difference the last time was that I was scared out of my mind. I couldn't have cared less that Margie accused me of being an alcoholic. She had accused me several times of being violent like my parents and dared me to hit her, which I never did. So I took her accusations with a grain of salt. It was the prospect of being homeless and not having a cent to my name that got my attention. I was evicted by my lover and incommunicado with my family. The few friends I had were drinking buddies, and they wouldn't give me any money nor take my dog and I in. I kept trying to think of someone that could help, but there was no one and nothing. In retrospect, I realize that I was actually very fortunate. My hard slide down to bottom got my attention. If I would have had anything or anyone left, I would have latched onto it like a life preserver. With absolutely nothing left, I had to make up with God. It couldn't be characterized as a happy reunion, at least on my part. I felt like I was in a game with no turns left and God kept rolling the dice and moving around the board. The line from *Jesus Christ Superstar* kept resounding through my head: "God, thy Will is hard, but you hold every card." I was definitely a far cry from a Galilean carpenter, but I thought that I knew how he felt.

It took almost a week to detox and to begin to feel somewhat normal. It was a strange sensation. It had been years since I hadn't had some level of alcohol in my system. I wouldn't say that it felt good, but nor would I say that it felt bad. It sure as hell felt different.

I had no money and no insurance, so considered myself ineligible for rehab. I also had no experience with social services, and was therefore clueless that there were resources available for people like me who are broke when they hit bottom. It didn't occur to me that most people at the end of their addiction aren't going to be driving up to a rehab center in a white Cadillac.

I white knuckled detox in the casket store. I shook a lot and often. When I wanted to drink, which was all the time, I ate ice cream – yet I still managed to lose over fifteen pounds of alcoholic bloat. With the loss of my two full-time jobs of drinking and yelling at Margie and the kids, I had a lot of time on my hands. I made friends again with my therapy buddies and tried to sell the caskets. Although I couldn't afford an apartment, let alone therapy, I still did therapy of a sort with my pals. I was surprised to find that talking about it helped me deal with the cravings.

My friends advised me that if I were serious about not drinking, I would have to do some things that I'd rather not do, one of which was to establish a relationship with God. I was less than thrilled about the prospect. Although I'd prayed to leave IBM, and then to go back, I had subsequently decided that God wasn't doing me any favors and had turned my back again. From my perspective, God was a prankster who took delight in shoving sticks in the wheel spokes of my life. Just look at the mess of my life. My buddies listened to my rants and then asked me to keep an open mind about it. Fortunately, they left it at that.

Although the physical cravings were gone in about a week, the emotional loss of losing alcohol was devastating. It was worse than any other loss I'd ever experienced, including the death of Mary Pat and my grandmother. Alcohol had been my one and only: my best friend, lover, family, and my solace. My entire world was gone and the grief was tremendous.

Despite my bereavement and shaky sobriety, the practical matter of dealing with the mess of my life demanded immediate attention. I had to give up the casket store within the month. I sold the caskets for pennies on the dollar to local funeral directors, who descended on the stock like locusts. My stomach churned as I watched them truck the caskets away. I felt like I had let my family down. One of the undertakers turned to me on the way out.

"Expensive experiment, eh?" he leered at me.

"Go fuck yourself, asshole." He'd given me cash. I had nothing to lose.

I was fortunate that the building owner was as good as his word and let me out of the lease. You can't get blood out of a rock, but I had enough on my hands without the legal trouble and credit hit of a broken lease. The lease release was a godsend. Unemployable, I would live on credit card advances for the next year. The American economic system is amazing. Just make the minimum payment and you can go on for a long time with no verifiable income. As Rita Mae Brown once said: "Education is a wonderful thing. If you couldn't sign your name you'd have to pay cash."

Meg, a friend of a friend, let me live with her for a couple of months until one of the cheap apartments in her complex became vacant. My 100-pound Malamute completely trashed her house one day and she still let me stay. I will never forget her kindness, as I would have been homeless otherwise.

I looked for a job during the day and walked my dog in the evenings. During those nights, I let God have it to make up for all those years that we were incommunicado, and I had a lot to say. In pre-bag-lady style, I ranted at God as I walked my dog down the littered city streets of my neighborhood that hadn't seen good days in a long time. As I ranted, I gave Him the finger. God was a Him, as far as I was concerned. A female God wouldn't be such a prick. I was livid at being born, livid at my life, livid that I wasn't drinking and livid that I was alive. Every bit of this was God's fault; I took zero responsibility. Although I walked past plenty of people, nobody stared and nobody bothered me. Apparently, people wandering around Fort Lauderdale yelling at God at the top of their lungs wasn't something out of the ordinary.

One of my friends called one evening to let me know that she'd found me a job. I was ecstatic! I could hardly wait to go back to big tech and start paying off the mounting bills. When I sobered up, I realized that my credit cards were worse off than I originally thought.

I had about thirty thousand dollars' worth of credit card debt that I hadn't noticed while I was drinking.

"That's great!" I enthused. Jan's girlfriend had worked for IBM as well. I assumed that she had connections to another tech company. This was going to be good! I could already see myself back into a nice house and out of my shitty ghetto apartment.

"It's at my bakery. I was there this morning and saw a Help Wanted sign in the front, so I told them my friend was looking for a job."

Jan went on to describe the location, but I had stopped listening at "bakery". Bakery? Bakery! What the fuck? I was an engineer. An engineer with a business degree! She was out of her mind for even suggesting such a thing.

I had a momentary lapse into sanity and found the presence of mind to thank Jan for thinking of me and managed to hang up without slamming the phone down. I sunk down on the threadbare, sagging couch that should have been tossed into a landfill three hand-me-downs ago. I felt as rode hard as the couch looked. I looked around at my decrepit 10' x 10' living room containing all of my worldly possessions: the aging couch, a thirteen inch black and white television, a stereo, and a brass stand that was used to exhibit urns in the casket store. The only thing left of any value was the stereo, and even that wouldn't get much at the pawn shop.

I wanted to punch someone in the head. Had I quit drinking just to wind up working in a bakery like Grandpy the Terrible? What was next? Would I wake up to find myself with a part-time job in a day care, dishing up limburger surprise for the kiddies? My whole life continued to spin out of control like a mad ghost was at the helm. Jesus H. Christ, could I use a drink. Instead, I shoved some Blue Ribbon chocolate ice cream in my face, leashed up my dog Ruger, and went for my nightly walk. As I walked, I cursed at God more than usual.

"Happy? Happy now, motherfucker?" I raged, shaking my fist at the sky and shooting my middle finger upward as hard as I could. The person that I wanted to punch in the head was God. One good punch, right in His you-can't-see-me, know-it-all, stupid face. As I walked and screamed, I slowly began to calm down, as I did every night. I returned back to the small compound that held Meg's tiny house and the microscopic apartment and decided that this might be a good job for now. Maybe a putsy bakery job would be just what I needed. It wouldn't be stressful, and maybe I could score some free cookies. I'd never been one for any sugar that wasn't accompanied by alcohol, but I'd developed a major sweet tooth since my breakup with booze.

I got up the next morning, dressed up in my best IBM suit and set off for the bakery. Despite my resolve of the previous night that a bakery job would be best, my resolution had somehow dissolved during the night. I sobbed during the whole drive and had to pull the car over several times, as I couldn't see through the tears. I was devastated. I could have stayed in Erie, PA and worked in a bakery. Then I could drink all day for the rest of my life like my relatives did. All that work to improve my life had amounted to nothing. I was the family's biggest loser, and that was some serious losing.

Pulling into the parking lot of the bakery, I took a deep breath to pull myself together. Feeling better after a few minutes, I killed the ignition on the Mazda and used the rearview mirror to throw some makeup on. As I got out of the car, I checked to ensure that my necklace was straight against my black blouse. I checked my red suit for lint and marched in black pumps across the parking lot into the bakery. The chunky, auburn haired woman behind the counter smiled pleasantly as I walked in.

"Hi, I'm looking for the manager."

"Yes?" She looked at me expectantly.

"My friend mentioned that I'd be coming by. I'm here about the job?" I pointed to the Help Wanted sign in the window.

Her eyebrows furrowed slightly as she checked out the red suit. "Do you have any experience?"

"Experience? What kind of experience?" I couldn't believe my ears. I had expected immediate recognition of my superior abilities.

"Bakery experience," she said patiently.

"Experience," I said incredulously. "I put the rolls in the bag, they give me money. Then I give them their change and rolls." My engineering brain logically broke the steps down as though I were explaining a highly technical process to a dolt. Then I pounded the final nail into the coffin. "How hard can it be?"

Her smile froze. "I'll call you."

I waved as I walked out the door and as it closed behind me, I was hit with a sudden realization. She hadn't asked for my number. I sobbed in the parking lot for a long time before I could finally drive away. I couldn't even get a job in a bakery; I was a bigger loser than even the crazy old German.

After I'd been sober around six months, I decided to tell Beth that I had quit drinking. I hadn't spoken to her much in the final years of my drinking and she had no idea how bad it had gotten. She called one evening and I stopped during the conversation to take a sip of iced tea. Over the phone, she heard the ice cubes clinking against the glass.

"Having a nice gin and tonic?" she asked.

"Um. No. I don't do that anymore."

"You don't do what?" She was puzzled. Everyone thought that I would drink gin and tonic until I died. I almost did.

"I don't drink."

"Why not?"

"Because I'm like them. Gertie and Wild Bill. You know, an alcoholic."

"Shut up! You are not like them! Why do you say that? Tell me one thing that makes you think that you're an alcoholic," she demanded.

"I kept airplane bottles of booze in the wheel well of my car."

"What? Why did you do that?"

"Because it's very efficient. I could store a lot of them, chug them in a hurry, and no one would look there. Have you ever heard of anyone else doing that?" I didn't want to tell her about all of the mini bottles that Margie had found. She was quiet for a moment.

"Huh. You may have something there."

I went on to tell her about closing the casket store and my tiny two room apartment.

"Too bad," she mused. "You had the world by the ass."

I didn't need her to remind me. I reminded myself every minute of every day.

My father passed away after I'd been sober for about a year. Although I hadn't seen him in over ten years, I flew up to Erie for his funeral. He'd been living in a small motel on the edge of town and had been dead for three days before the motel manager broke in to check on him. Wild Bill was found on his knees by the side of his bed in the cheap motel room where he'd lived in virtual isolation for three years. An empty whiskey bottle was on one side of him and an open Bible on the other. There was never a starker example of a man conflicted over which god to serve, nor which one won.

Beth called on a chilly Saturday morning in March to break the news. "The Old Man died." No need to be gentle, there was no love lost on any of our parts.

My practical engineering side immediately kicked in. "Don't finalize the funeral arrangements until I get there," I instructed, still the bossy big sister. I was still smarting from the financial beating that I'd taken at the hands of the funeral industry and was eager to throw a few punches back. Besides, Beth was pregnant and I was afraid that she would be no match for the experienced undertaker who had already helped himself to more of our money than he should have. As it turned out, I was right to be worried.

When I met Beth in the only terminal of the Erie airport, she announced that there was no need to worry; she had taken care of the funeral arrangements. Sobriety had done little to curb my quick temper, but I had at least begun to have a modicum of control over it – far more control than I'd ever had before. So I said as mildly as I could, "How about if I give him a call when we get to your house?"

When I got the undertaker on the phone, I introduced myself and cut right to the chase. "David, we're not paying $4,000 for my father's funeral."

"Ms. Frombach, I know that you're upset. It's understandable, as you've just suffered a terrible loss." Oozing bullshit, his first line of defense was artificial soothing.

"Are you available? I'd like to come over and discuss what items will be removed from the contract." Beth had told me that he lived right behind the funeral home, so I knew he was close by.

"Your sister has already signed the bill for our services," he reminded me, his professional silky voice not quite as syrupy this time. He'd toughened up when he realized that I'd spit out the hook.

"I'll meet you at your office in ten minutes." I hung up and ran out the door, grabbing Beth's car keys on the way out. It was nine o'clock on a Sunday night and I reveled in the thought that I'd caught him off guard. He wasn't expecting this tactic from a grieving customer. When I got to his office, he barely had control of his professional demeanor.

"See here, Ms. Frombach, we have a signed contract. I know that you're upset, but your father wouldn't have wanted things handled in this manner."

"Rip up the contract. My father left no will and no instructions. So unless you're a medium, you have no idea of what he wanted. Besides, his days of telling anyone what he wants and doesn't want are long gone. I also don't appreciate your taking advantage of my sister when she's pregnant." I finally had a target for my fury and it was sweeter yet that he was in the brotherhood of undertakers. I'd been ripped off by the funeral industry enough.

"We can't rip up the contract. He's already been embalmed, according to state law," he said, trying to misdirect me.

"But he hasn't been buried yet, has he?" I happily countered.

"No. No, he hasn't," he said through tight lips.

"Good. Then we'll eat the cost of the embalming, but he is going to be cremated, not buried. We won't need a casket, and since we won't need a casket, we won't need a burial vault. You can also remove the hearse, driver, prayer cards, and greeter." Sitting in his stately office in sweater and jeans, David scowled at me with barely concealed fury. I looked directly at him and smiled.

By the time we were done, the cost was just under $2,000, exactly the amount of the pre-need contract that Beth had taken out on him years ago. My father was sixty years old when he died of alcoholism and we were surprised that he had lasted that long. But we also had another card up our sleeve for David. Wild Bill had received a social security check that he hadn't yet cashed. Beth knew that social security checks were worthless, except for funeral expenses. So we used the check for his headstone and had just enough left over to buy for a headstone for Mary Pat, who had been gone six years. My father did in death what he'd never once considered in life; he bought his daughter a headstone.

CHAPTER NINETEEN

2007

Sitting on the living room floor next to the Christmas tree, I carefully wrapped the last-minute Christmas gifts. This Christmas Eve morning marked my sixth sober holiday season, and I was a far different person than the one who had stared at the camera with bloodless eyes that Christmas morning at Margie's house. After years at dead end jobs, I'd worked hard to earn additional IT certifications and had recently begun working as a contractor for Xerox. I had the whole holiday week off with pay for the first time since I'd left IBM. The ship of my life had begun righting itself again in many ways and I had dramatically changed at every level. I had lost the alcoholic bloat, made a sizeable dent in the drinking debt that I'd accrued, and had continued to work on myself in therapy. At my therapist's suggestion, I had even started talking to my mother. Oh, sure, there were still occasional screaming meltdowns and a road rage incident now and again, but who didn't have a bad day sometimes? Just because I'd quit drinking didn't mean that I'd turned into a saint.

It was hot in South Florida that holiday season, so the air conditioning carried the scent of the simmering mulling spices throughout the house. In a festive holiday mood, I hummed along to Christmas carols on the stereo and carefully applied tape to the last gift. No gift wrapper by nature, I was having fun with it that day. The ringing of the phone interrupted Karen Carpenter encouraging me to have myself a merry little Christmas, and I wondered who the first holiday caller would be. I did my best impression of a Santa imitation.

"Ho, Ho, Ho, Merry Christmas!"

"Hey." Beth clearly wasn't feeling the holiday love.

"Hey, yourself. Is everything ok?"

"Trudy is on her way to the ER." Beth said flatly. My mother's given name was Gertrude. Both she and her sister had been named after aunts. Although named for her favorite aunt, my mother had definitely gotten the short end of the naming stick. After she'd retired, she'd inexplicably shed her hated childhood name of Gertie, and had taken to calling herself Trudy. Beth and I thought that she should have ditched both old-timey names and called herself Mary, but she'd latched on to Trudy and stuck to it like a Kardashian to the front of a camera. We obliged her by calling her Trudy as well.

"Goddamn it. Merry Fucking Christmas. What the hell is she going to the hospital for?" I'd thought that the days of my parents fucking up yet another holiday season were O V E R. Evidently, I thought W R O N G.

"She can't breathe and she's been retaining fluid for almost a week. She called the paramedics to take her to the ER." Beth and her family had moved to Memphis and my mother still lived in Erie. She had never learned to drive, didn't have a car, and had no one that she could count on for transportation since Beth left.

After smoking two packs of cigarettes a day for over thirty-five years, Trudy had been diagnosed with emphysema or Chronic Obstructive Pulmonary Disease (COPD) several years before. Fluid had been drained out of her lungs numerous times and her doctor warned her that she was signing her own death certificate if she continued to smoke. She dutifully agreed with him that she needed to quit and meekly assured him that she would. Her strong resolve lasted the five minutes that it took to get wheeled to the hospital exit. Just outside the door, she stopped the nurse pushing her wheelchair long enough to dig out the spare pack of ciggy butts hidden in her purse and promptly lit up.

After I'd been sober for almost five years, June had suggested that I contact my mother. I'd been in therapy with June for almost the entire time I'd been sober and trusted her implicitly, a trust which I began to doubt at that moment.

“Are you out of your fucking mind? Why would I contact her?” I wondered if June realized how close to death she was at that moment. With wavy blonde hair and a strong resemblance to self-help guru and former model Louise Hay, June could still turn heads, male and female. She kept herself up and you couldn’t guess her age if you had a gun to your head. She was somewhere between sixty and ninety. I would feel bad for killing an old lady, but she certainly deserved it for suggesting that I call my mother. Stone cold sober, I can’t kill bugs...but interestingly, sometimes indulging in violent thoughts was the only remedy that quelled the urge to act on them; a built-in emotional safety valve of sorts. The fact that I eventually allowed both of my parents to die of natural causes is proof positive that the safety valve had been successful for many years. In my mind, I had killed them dozens of times. Obviously, I wasn’t in prison because I had somehow retained a modicum of self-control, no matter how drunk I was.

“Because, darling, it’s time.” June called everyone darling.

“Time for what?”

“Time to forgive her. It’s time to forgive both of your parents, really. But your mother is still alive and I *strongly* suggest that you reach out so that you can begin to develop a relationship with her.” June’s sky-blue eyes locked directly on mine as I gaped at her. She waited for the explosion. It was immediate.

“There is no fucking way. NO. FUCKING. WAY.” I shot up from the couch in her office as though an electric current had just crossed it. Livid, I didn’t know whether to put my car keys through her temple or my own. Maybe the safety valve wasn’t going to work this time.

“This is unadulterated bullshit! Do you hear me? Bullshit!” I screamed. I felt the veins on my neck straining against my skin. “After what they did to me growing up? Fuck her! Fuck them, god damn it. Go fuck yourself too, while you’re at it. Fuck all of this.” I threw my keys down on the beige carpet. I had great respect for June and had never acted out with her. Despite my rage, part of me was stunned that I was screaming at her, but I couldn’t help it. I thought that my mind was going to snap.

"I know, darling," she almost whispered, in stark contrast to my yelling. Her eyes hadn't budged, staying on me.

I turned toward the door to leave. Then, I collapsed back onto the couch in tears.

"You have no idea what it was like. No one does," I sobbed. Long, hot tears ran down my face. I covered my face with one of the brown sofa pillows. I wanted to die. I hadn't cried in years, and was embarrassed that there was a witness.

"There is n-n-n-no way I can f-f-f-f-forgive them. I c-c-c-can't. Na-never. Tha-they-they, they da-did things ya-you d-d-ddon't know about. Tha-tha-things I've n-n-n-never told anyone." I sobbed convulsively and buried my head in my arms. I could hardly breathe.

June sat impassively in her seat. She didn't move or speak. She waited until I calmed down. I uncovered my face. Snot streaming out of my nose, I grabbed the ubiquitous Kleenex box. I managed to look up at her. She remained silent for a moment, watching me, seemingly lost in thought. When she did speak, her voice was so soft that I had to lean forward to hear her.

"It will be hard, darling. The hardest thing you've ever done. But do it, you must."

"Why? Why?" I wailed. "I just need to forget. Forget her. Forget them. Forget all of it."

"You drank to forget, but it didn't work, did it? If you don't forgive her, forgive both of them, then you *will* drink again."

I slumped against the back of the couch. Her eyes still on me, her low, soft voice went on. "You might not drink tomorrow, nor maybe next year. But drink, you will. And, if you drink again, there is no guarantee that you will be able to stop the next time. Then, you will destroy yourself. You will succeed at destroying yourself where they failed to." She stopped and sat silently to let me absorb the enormity of the truth of what she had just said. We sat in absolute silence for a long while. June had been sober for over thirty years, so she had a lot of street cred from my perspective. I wouldn't have taken that shit from anyone else. Alcoholism wasn't a theory out of a book for her, she knew the score. A part of me knew she was right, although I absolutely couldn't stand even the thought of it. I finally broke the silence.

"THEY are NOT going to win. I can do this. I don't want to, but I will," I told her very calmly, a striking contrast to my hysteria of a few moments ago. I looked past her into the far distance. I'd said the words, which was a huge step for me, but I felt nothing by that point. I had spaced out. I was a space cadet, far away inside my head.

I floated in a place with neither time nor limits. A special place where nothing could touch me or hurt me. It was like being in outer space, only it was inside of me, my own domain. My internal view was as breathtaking and spacious as any vista that NASA has documented. All of that space gave me an immense barrier from the world. I was not unconscious, or unaware of what was going on around me. I was always aware of my physical surroundings, even if that awareness was only secured by a tiny thread. I just did not give the slightest fuck about anything in the physical world while I was spaced out.

I needed to be thousands of miles away to even consider June's suggestion. I needed to be in my familiar space, my safe haven. It was where I had lived for most of my life. I could be still there, very still. I smiled slightly. My little secret. No one ever knew when I was there. I sometimes didn't know, myself. It often happened automatically, as it just had. I would just find myself there. It didn't matter whether I took myself there or it happened on its own. All that mattered was that my secret universe existed, that it was always available to me, and that no one could ever take it away. My spaceship was my physical self, which I often left on autopilot while I floated. I was fortunate that I hadn't killed myself from neglect.

June suggested that I call my mother every Saturday morning to establish a pattern of communication. Trudy wouldn't be sober, but she would be less drunk in the morning than at any other time. Since she usually didn't start drinking 'til noon, there was a small window of opportunity. She typically got up around nine and would be slightly hung-over, but still a half day away from an alcohol-fueled full-on nasty zenith. So between ten and ten thirty every Saturday morning, I obliged June and prepped for the call. I'd lay out my magazine for the week and slowly pick up the phone as though it weighed ten tons. As I dialed, I intentionally spaced out so that I was already floating by the time she answered.

If she was surprised to hear from me after so many years, she never mentioned it. You would have thought that nothing had ever happened between mother and daughter. But that's the way of the alcoholic family, isn't it? To pretend that nothing ever happened? Since she hadn't had the first Gennie of the day yet, she would actually attempt to be nice at times, carrying on about the weather or something else equally as innocuous. I would sit at the other end of the line, grunting from time to time and paging through Time or Newsweek. The calls never went on for more than ten minutes, which was all of the mother and child relationship building that I could handle for one sitting. Besides, I read quickly and was done with the magazine after ten minutes.

I would report back to June every week: yes, I called. Yes, we talked. Yes, I'll call her again this weekend. I didn't see the point to any of it. I was no closer to forgiveness. I still hated her. My butthole puckered every time I even heard her voice. June assured me that I was making progress, although I had no idea what that meant. I actually felt more like drinking than not on those Saturday mornings. But I'd space out, call someone, or have some marshmallows with their pure sugar payload and the feeling would pass. I reminded myself that if I drank, THEY won. That wasn't going to happen. Not again.

I didn't mention my floating secret to June. It wasn't that I was trying to keep it from her, it just didn't occur to me. I had no point of reference. I thought that everyone floated. I thought that everyone retreated to their special place whenever it all got to be too much. I couldn't imagine how anyone could go through life without their own inner universe. The secret was that no one knew when I was there. I could be here and be there at the same time, but in retrospect, I was *there* far more often than I was *here*.

"Hey, are you there?" Beth's voice brought me back. I heard John Lennon singing "*So this is Christmas.*"

"Yeah, sorry. I spaced out for a minute."

CHAPTER TWENTY

Walking down the hospital corridor on Christmas Day, I steeled myself for my first encounter with my mother in years. Head held high, I almost assumed my old military bearing. My demeanor shouted to any observer: I mean business, this means you! When under attack, many animals puff themselves up to look larger than they are. When a toad senses a snake, the toad stretches its legs and inflates itself to three times its normal size. Snakes can't swallow such a large toad, so they move on. I couldn't super-inflate to triple my size, but I could take a deep breath to look my imposing best as I stepped into the hospital room. I marched into Trudy's room with puffed chest and squared shoulders – and stopped short in mid-stride. No need for puffery in that room. Enveloped by monitors and tubes, my mother was a shadow of the dragon that I remembered. Lying behind the rails of the institutional grey hospital bed, she looked like a shrunken Auschwitz victim. At five foot five, Trudy had weighed in to the ER at eighty-five pounds. Her wide brown eyes swam in dark pools of sunken eye sockets. Light grey skin covered purple veins that still showed a pulse, the only indicator that the skeletal frame in front of me didn't belong in a graveyard. The blue hospital gown allowed no denial of the living cadaver that I faced. Beth had spoken to the nurse after Trudy had been admitted and warned me that Trudy was underweight, but nothing could have prepared me for this sight. The staff in the ER had discovered that my mother wore pajamas under her clothes. The obvious reason was to keep her warm during the frigid Erie winter, but the real reason was so that people wouldn't see how much weight she'd lost. Which people she was worried about was a mystery; at this point, the only person that my mother saw on a regular basis was the guy who delivered the beer. Since her retirement, she had virtually stopped eating, choosing instead to sit in front of the television drinking beer and smoking cigarettes all day. Aside from the TV, it was a pattern that I was personally familiar with.

"Got a cigarette on you?" she whined plaintively as I stared at her. No greeting. No hello. No "how've you been for the last ten years?" No "thanks for dropping all of your holiday plans and driving twenty-four hours." Same shit, different day.

"Excuse me?"

"The nurses took my ciggy butts out of my purse. I'll just go into the bathroom and have a quick one. I don't care what kind they are."

"Um. Huh. Did it occur to you that the combination of fire and that oxygen mask on your face could blow you and everyone else within shouting distance to kingdom come?" Still in business mode, I was surprisingly calm, but every fiber of my being wanted to turn right around and go back to Florida. I spaced out instead.

"Really? Ok, then I'll leave the mask here on the bed. Do you have a butt?"

"No, I don't smoke anymore."

She looked crestfallen and turned back toward the television on the wall. Her doctor walked in.

"How are we doing?" He nodded toward me and motioned toward the hallway. I followed him out to the hall and propped myself against the grey wall for support.

He got right to the point. "How much does she drink every day?"

"Who knows? She lives by herself. What's her prognosis?"

"She told me that she only has a couple of beers a day, but her body tells a different story. She has congestive heart failure complicated by COPD and chronic starvation." He waited for my reaction and when I didn't have one, he continued. "She's drinking instead of eating and it's affected her thinking. Your mother is in major denial about her situation. She may improve slightly, but I have to tell you that her long-term prognosis isn't good."

I nodded. "I'm a recovering alcoholic myself, so I get it. We've begged her for thirty years to quit smoking. I'm surprised that she's held out this long."

His raised eyebrows indicated agreement. He said, "We've done all we can for her here. We'll move her to a rehab so that she can get some physical therapy, but she can't live by herself any longer."

I called Beth from the pay phone in the hospital lobby. We'd discussed the strategy before I left Florida: I would drive to Pennsylvania and assess the situation. Like anyone in any profession, medical staff seems to be a little more responsive when you're nose to nose with them. Beth didn't want to ruin her kid's Christmas and I didn't blame her a bit. There was no sense in both of us having another ruined holiday, so I'd be the squeaky wheel and we'd go from there.

"Not good," I told her when she answered the phone. I briefed her on the situation and was surprised to hear myself say that I could stay for a few more days until Trudy was settled in rehab. It was almost surreal. I hated my mother, and her pathetic situation hadn't altered my hatred one iota, yet I found myself willing to help her out. If you had bet me the day before Christmas Eve that I would cross the street to help my mother, let alone drive fifteen hundred miles, I would have considered it easy money. But I found myself sitting next to her bed in the rehab unit, on the losing side of the bet.

As her advocate in rehab, I observed my mother and her health through safety of my floating cloud. Floating didn't make me any less effective at taking care of business; I'd been doing it all my life. It was very strange to see the woman who had terrorized me and many others over the years reduced to an invalid. I expected her to leap out of bed at any moment, chase me down the hall, and pin my shoulders to the floor.

"Surprise! I fooled ya. Eh, Sis?" she'd scream in my face with a feral grin, just like old times.

I kept a safe distance from her bed, just in case. I always had my eye on her, even when she thought that I wasn't looking. Old habits die hard.

The doctor wasn't exaggerating. Over the next several days, it became obvious that Trudy was in no condition to live by herself. She required an oxygen machine and could only get out of bed and shuffle around for a while on good days. Since she was unwillingly separated from her lifelong friends of Gennie and ciggies, she was completely listless. It was as though her spirit was keeping step with her declining body in preparing to leave this life. She was in grief for her lost friends. They were all that she'd had for so long that when they were gone, she was bereft. In shock, and lacking other coping skills or resources, she had no other choice but to await their return. Not unlike best friends who had gone shopping and stayed at the mall a little too long, they might be back any minute. During her wait, she had no interest in participating in her own recovery and had to be cajoled and bribed with candy to engage in physical therapy. Alcohol contains a lot of sugar, and since she couldn't have booze, she craved sweets. Like most alcoholics, her personality was completely different without alcohol in her system. No anger. No rage. No razor blade mouth. She still wasn't anyone's version of a sweet little old lady, but the sharpest part of her edge had dulled.

Trudy's insurance would pay for rehab for at least a couple of months, but long-term care was a question mark. Her response to any question regarding her preference or plan was a blank stare or shrug of the shoulders. It was as though we were asking her about a stranger. She was seemingly indifferent to any plan besides returning home. Evidently, I wasn't the only one in the family in my own universe. At any rate, my job was done. Mission accomplished. I'd helped my mother in her hour of need before she passed away. Proud of myself for my final grand gesture of service to the person that I loathed most, I left Trudy to her rehab and gladly returned to Florida to resume my interrupted life.

CHAPTER TWENTY-ONE

1998

Even though I'd become accustomed to those Saturday morning phone calls with Trudy, it didn't get any easier to go through with them. I still dreaded them and still broke out in a rash right before I called her. Taking a couple of deep breaths, I dialed the number of my mother's rehab and waited to be connected to her room. She picked up on the first ring.

"Hey, how's it going?" Thumbing through this weeks' *Time* magazine, I idly wondered if Hillary would actually run for the Senate from New York. No chance, I concluded.

"Pretty good. How's by you?" Trudy had been surprisingly chipper since she'd been in rehab. No complaining. No whining. No snarky remarks. Like many alcoholics, she experienced a personality transplant when she hadn't been drinking for a while. No one would ever accuse her of being Pollyanna, but she surprisingly hadn't complained since she'd been hospitalized. She'd been grousing about her life and everything in it ever since I could remember, so I still kept waiting for the other shoe to drop. This new mother would take some getting used to.

She particularly surprised everyone, perhaps even herself, by not dying. After seeing her in the hospital, I couldn't imagine how she'd lived this long. Every time the phone rang, I expected to hear the hushed voice of a stranger informing me that my mother had passed. But Trudy had no intention of going anywhere. If she'd had any familiarity with the works of Mark Twain, she would have reminded us that "the reports of her death were greatly exaggerated."

Proving that you can go a long way on sheer spite, she did more than spit in the face of the grim reaper: her health actually improved. With regular meals and physical therapy, she had backed herself away from heaven's door for the time being. Having seen her living skeleton in the hospital, I wouldn't have believed anyone could survive a health crisis of that magnitude if I hadn't seen it for myself.

"Tee, hee, hee!" Trudy's childish giggle brought me back from Hillary's Senate aspirations. Through the phone, I heard my mother clapping her hands with delight. Her inner child had come out to play. I instinctively rolled my eyes and grabbed a handful of my own hair as though I could latch on to hers by proxy. Christ on the cross, how I loathed that brat.

"Now what?" I asked in a studiously bored voice, buried deep in inner space to control my anger. The Imp was my mother's inner child and hearing her callow voice never failed to trigger my rage. I had to float away as inward as possible to refrain from using the phone as a hammer on the tile floor. I shoved the heel of my hand in my mouth as hard as I could to control my compulsion to scream at her. I shook with the effort of muting myself from shrieking at her to shut the fuck up and grow the fuck up. Jesus, no wonder I drank. For the umpteenth time, I considered the irony that the solution for some of these situations seemed to be the same substance that caused them in the first place. My alcoholic family drove me crazy enough to think that a drink was the only thing that seemed like it would help. Insane thinking, for sure. But damn, I wanted a drink.

"Harriet found the spoon! I put it under the pillow and she found it!" Trudy squealed with delight like a child on Christmas morning. Harriet was her favorite nurse, and my mother demonstrated her affection by playing small tricks on her.

I silently prayed for Harriet to retrieve the spoon and replace it with my mother's face under the pillow for about five minutes. I comforted myself by visualizing that scenario as a scene in a movie. Harriet could be played by Joan Crawford. I thought it would be a fun twist on Mommy Dearest.

Between a rock and hard place, my mother did what she'd always done – regressed into fantasy land. She delighted herself by pretending rehab was a destination vacation or amusement park, providing playmates for her endless childish pranks. She thrived on the attention and loved being waited on as though she were royalty. All she needed to complete the scenario was a small bell to summon the mice footmen.

"Gail just checked in on me. She's just a bit of a thing, her husband worked with Twyla's husband over at Lord Manufacturing on Twelfth Street. We used to have the best time making fun of ol' Fart Face behind his back." Giggling at the memory, she rambled on in stream of consciousness chattering, hopping from subject to subject as though she were mentally skipping on rocks to cross that stream. Inevitably, like all children, the Imp related all topics to herself. Through years of practice, I could keep up with her mental gymnastics and connected the dots: Gail was one of the other nurses. I also dimly remembered that Twyla was a former colleague and ol' Fart Face was their manager. Emotionally spent after only a few minutes, I laid the phone on the sofa so that no words were distinguishable. This conversation was going nowhere, and obviously, neither was my work on forgiveness.

Chatty though Trudy might be about trivia, she clammed right up when pressed for details about the most immediate situation: her health. A surefire method to ending her prattling, dead silence greeted every inquiry into her diagnosis or progress. Whenever I spoke with the rehab medical staff, they were cautiously optimistic but revealed little real information. At the end of the day, my mother's insurance company was the best indicator of her condition. She'd reached a steady plateau, so her benefits were terminated.

I remained rooted to the couch long after I hung up the phone. With characteristic social worker enthusiasm, the case manager had broken the news that no one could have predicted three months prior: Trudy was being released from rehab. Her case worker carefully explained that my mother could walk for a few feet if she took her time, but climbing any stairs was out of the question. In other words, Trudy could no longer live in her two-story house. Even worse, she would require twenty-four hour monitoring and assistance. Her lungs could fill with fluid at any time and with the lack of oxygen, my mother would be unaware of her own crisis. But the rehab had gotten her to the point where she could at least get out of bed. Mission accomplished. The case worker did her best to soften the message, but it was essentially the same as any bar at closing time: your mother doesn't have to go home, but she can't stay here.

I stared out of the window at the beautiful spring day and shivered involuntarily despite the bright sunshine. Now what? The question of my mother's future loomed over Beth and I like the Sword of Damocles. Trudy was happily residing on Planet Denial, refusing to even acknowledge her situation. Like a child who covers her eyes and thinks that you can't see her, she played hide and seek with her life. She put far more thought into pranking the nurses than to where and how she was going to live. Someone else would take care of it; they always did. It didn't trouble her in the least that the "someone else" was inevitably one or both of her daughters.

We had no idea what resources my mother had, if any. She could have had a million dollars to her name or a hundred, it wouldn't have surprised us either way. Frugal by nature, she could pinch a nickel 'til the buffalo shit. But beer and cigarettes are expensive and demanding taskmasters. She had just started collecting social security, but that meager amount wouldn't touch the cost of a nursing home. My head hurt, an anvil banging with the hammer of resentment. How in the hell had I gotten involved in all of this? I silently cursed June. Fuck this forgiveness crap. That bullshit had launched me onto the entrance ramp of this highway to hell. The ringing of the phone startled me out of my "Fuck Therapy" mantra.

"I have an idea," Beth announced. Her tone made it clear that it was not a great idea, but options were in short supply at the moment so any idea would be great.

"What is it?" I asked suspiciously.

"Trudy can live here."

"Live where?" Stupefied, I had no idea what she was talking about. Was Beth visiting someone? Had Aunt Kay inexplicably lost her mind? What the hell was going on?

"Live with me."

If you were feeling generous, you would have estimated Beth's house to be around a thousand square feet. It was a cute three bedroom, two bath ranch-style home. But with two active children and three dogs, there was already barely enough room in the house for Beth to change her mind, let alone add a high-maintenance invalid with an entitlement disorder.

"You've lost your mind." Stunned, I couldn't even drop an F-bomb.

"Do you have any better suggestions?" Beth demanded.

"Maybe she could go to a nursing home...or somewhere." My voice trailed off. I sounded lame, even to myself. Neither of us had much money. I had just gotten a decent job, but still had a mountain of debt. Beth was a single mom raising two kids. We could sell Trudy's house, but alcoholics are as big on home upkeep as they are on personal maintenance, and my mother had been no exception. Her house would require a lot of work and she wouldn't get much for it. Three or four months in a nursing home would wipe out the proceeds. Then what? I was weary of thinking about it and my resentment migraine clanged louder. Every thought in my head seemed to have been assigned to its own hamster wheel – running, running, going nowhere.

Beth's silence punctuated the absurdity of my suggestion. There was really no other way. I inhaled and released my breath with a sigh.

"No. No. I don't have any other suggestions," I said quietly. It was an admission of utter failure. I had made a living for years solving complex computer problems, but had no solution to disentangle my sister and me from this Gordian knot that we'd never signed up for.

Neither of us mentioned it at the time, but it would have been absolutely convenient to leave my mother to her own devices, to reap what she had sown. As we grew up, she'd often repeated the old German idiom: "You made your bed, now lay in it." Trudy and her drunken viciousness had alienated almost everyone in her orbit. Very few people, if any, would have faulted Beth or me if we had gone on with our lives, leaving our mother to lay in the bed that she'd made over the years. With her alcoholism and mental illness, my mother had abandoned and abused Beth and I countless times in almost every way imaginable. But although we never discussed it, my sister and I intrinsically knew that retaliation wasn't our path. We heard another call, if you will. It wasn't a call that made me happy in the least, but it was a call that I obeyed. I no longer walked my dog down the street giving God the finger, but I would look up sometimes during those days and ask, "Are you fucking kidding me? She's been a douche to me. Why do I have to help her ass out? Fuck her and fuck you too." Then I'd go and do what intuitively felt like the next right thing, despite the fact that I was massively unhappy about it. It seemed as though God never asked me if I was going to be happy doing his will, He just wanted it done. So I did it. But I did it grudgingly, like a kid mowing the grass while all the other kids were at the playground. It seemed as though all of the other kids in the world were blithely going on with the playgrounds of their lives while Beth and I did the yard work. Both God and my mother were a royal pain in my ass.

As it turned out, Trudy did have a little money saved up; no small feat for someone on her income with Gennie and ciggy butt habits. As we suspected, she didn't have enough to afford a decent nursing home. However, she could at least afford to hire a medical jet to transport her from Erie to Memphis to live with Beth. I flew up to Beth's from Florida, under the pretense of helping my mother get settled. In reality, as an alcoholic, I knew how my mother was going to be when it hit her that she wouldn't be able to drink at Beth's and in fact could never drink again. Beth isn't an alcoholic and wouldn't understand the dynamics of a dry alcoholic. Trudy was going to throw a shitstorm of epic proportions and would require managing from someone who wasn't going to live with her. Having played the family bad cop for years, it was a role that I was weary of but familiar with. I readied myself for the ordeal.

One would think that someone in my mother's situation would have been grateful to have been spared the nursing home bullet. Indeed, all things considered, grateful to be alive at all. But we alcoholics are arrogant bastards and it takes a long, long time after we stop drinking to develop a sense of gratitude. Thankfulness is a skill and gift that develops gradually, and only if a person has the slightest interest in that path, which Trudy certainly did not. She entered my sister's home with an immense sense of entitlement, wiping her feet on gratitude at the front door.

Trudy had gotten hooked on having a lot of attention at the rehab, raising a ruckus at any given time to ensure that she got her fix. It was, perhaps, her primary addiction all along. Like any addict, she wasn't going to give it up without a fight. Like any single mother, Beth's life had been hectic even before my mother's crisis and she wouldn't have the time nor the inclination to play nursemaid. Since I wouldn't be going back to Florida for a few days, I would deal with Trudy's initial temper tantrums but wouldn't be around for long to feel the wrath of the Imp. In my mother's weakened state, I'd lost my terror of her physical presence, but the scars of her acid mouth would never vanish. I girded myself for battle.

My mother and I sat in Beth's small living room, which Trudy had turned into her domain. Her oxygen machine was in the corner, connected to a twenty foot plastic hose that delivered oxygen to her ubiquitous nose cannula, enabling mobility to the kitchen and bathroom. The couch was an unmade, makeshift bed strewn with wrinkled white sheets. Inhalers and over a dozen brown medication bottles covered one end table, while the other held Kleenex and other personal items. Some of her clothes were piled up at the end of the couch and her socks and slippers loosely formed a pyramid near one end of the couch to camouflage the candy bags stuffed underneath. It wasn't to make the couch look more presentable; Trudy just didn't want anyone to see her stash and steal it. I had gotten her two ten pound bags of candy as a welcome gift. Beth had thought that it was an odd gift, but I remembered my own sugar cravings immediately after I stopped drinking. I knew that the candy would keep Trudy somewhat sated, or at least as sated an alcoholic can be when they quit drinking involuntarily.

My mother was propped upright against two large pillows to enable her to breathe better. Her shapeless, ancient sweatshirt was inside out and she kept pulling up faded dungarees, which were at least a decade old and two sizes too large. With the worst case of bed head that I'd ever seen, her hair hadn't seen a brush since she left rehab. Staring at the television, Trudy shoveled Tootsie Rolls into her mouth and threw the white and brown wrappers on the floor. I could almost smell the lasagna that Beth had in the oven, but it was overpowered by the sickly sweet stench of the chronically ill. I sat in the rocking chair several feet away watching her for a few minutes as she ignored me. Then I raised my voice slightly so that she could hear me over of the blare of the TV and whir of the oxygen machine.

"You're going to have to clean those up," I said evenly. After a pause, I continued, "Actually, you're going to have to keep up after yourself while you're living here. Beth and the kids aren't going to have time to clean up after you."

Trudy continued staring at the screen as though I hadn't said a word. She leaned forward slowly and reached her claw under the couch to pull out another round of candy. Her eyes never left the television.

"Did you hear me?" I felt like an emotionless robot, and she certainly looked like one. The Imp turned toward me slowly and our eyes locked. Neither blinked. Blink first and lose. The primary rule of engagement for any negotiation.

"I heard you." She turned back toward Alex Trebek and threw another wrapper on the floor.

CHAPTER TWENTY-TWO

2001

Although I knew that my mother was going to be a handful when she realized that she would no longer be able to smoke or drink, I didn't know that a handful would be an understatement. I left Memphis in a deep funk. Both Beth and I had hoped that the absence of alcohol and her near-death experience would have left her with a new attitude. Although nothing she'd ever done so far in her life suggested that she'd be appreciative, anyone would have thought that a person in her position would be glad to be living with family. Many elderly in such situations are dumped at institutions by their relatives, like pets abandoned at the shelter entrance when they're no longer convenient.

Both of us had imagined that my mother would be on her best behavior, like she was in rehab. We thought that she'd at least pretend to be pleasant, the kind of fake affability you display on the first couple of dates or first week on the job. The kind that says, "I'm so glad to be here that I'm not going to be an asshole right away." But no, Trudy would be having none of that. Although she'd lost the sharp-edged nastiness of a full-on drunk, the Imp was ever-present and more demanding than any petulant child. Beth had signed up to care for an ailing parent who could do many things for herself, not a sulky child in a deteriorating body who manipulated her illness to be waited on. On the flight back to Fort Lauderdale, I couldn't stop thinking about Beth's situation and wished that there was something that I could do to help her.

Before I went to Memphis, I'd arranged for some job interviews at FedEx so that I could write the trip off on my taxes. Since my only purpose for the interviews was to avoid IRS penalties in the event of an audit, I completely forgot about them as soon as they were over. Preoccupied with Trudy's drama, I had spaced out on the interviews to the degree that when FedEx HR called, I thought it was a package notification. As it turned out, FedEx made me an extremely lucrative offer – for a Memphis-based position. If I didn't think that God had a sense of humor before, I became a believer that day. I looked up to the sky and shook my head. "Really, God? Really? You have got to be kidding." It quickly became apparent that God was indeed serious.

I looked forward to living in Memphis and being near my mother with as much enthusiasm as men look forward to passing a kidney stone. But FedEx offered me more money than I'd ever made in my life. The salary that they offered would enable me to quickly pay off the drinking debts that I still owed, six years after I'd gotten sober. But even more than the money, I felt deep down that moving to Memphis was something that I was supposed to do. In other words, God wanted me there and would pay me to go. I accepted the offer, rationalizing that Trudy couldn't last long in her condition.

I got an apartment a few miles from Beth's house and settled into life in the Deep South. In addition to mother shock, I also experienced a rude case of culture shock. South Florida is a melting pot of black, white, brown, Asian, Christian, Jewish, straight, gay, and everything in between. If you live there, you probably won't like everyone, but you can be assured that there are many, many people who are different from you and you will have to develop at least a modicum of tolerance. Locked in a 1950s mindset, Memphis never got that diversity memo.

Although I'd experienced covert anti-gay bigotry on occasion, I'd never observed outright prejudice in action until I got to Memphis. Shortly after I started at FedEx, I was chatting with several colleagues about some office gossip or other and was startled by a comment from a woman about my age.

"T.N.S.," she sneered.

"What does that mean?" I was puzzled as much by her sudden change in demeanor as by the acronym.

"Typical Niggah SHEEIT," she explained with a roll of the eyes, emphasizing for dramatic effect.

"That isn't very funny," I said automatically. It was the rudest joke that I'd ever heard.

"Oh, yeah. I forgot. We got a damn Florida Yankee here now." She rolled her eyes and sneered again.

It finally hit me: oh, my God. She wasn't joking.

At one time, Atlanta and Memphis were about the same size and had the same racial issues. But Atlanta blacks and whites realized that if they worked together, everyone could make a lot of green, which is everyone's favorite color. By contrast, Memphis has frozen in time, and so has its economy. While the city still convulses in prejudice and poverty, chasing its racist tail and relying on almost solely on FedEx to supply the city with jobs, Atlanta has become the biggest city in the South, pulling in the jack with thousands of corporations headquartered there. However, there is one population that Memphis blacks and whites seem to hate more than each other: gays. I felt like Dorothy who'd spun backwards from bright sparkly Oz to black-and-white Kansas, and the only one who'd come with me was the wicked witch.

Neither my mother nor I drank any longer, and I worked on forgiveness like a bitch, but I still hated her with a passion. I tried talking to her, praying for her, writing letters that I never sent, but it still seemed as though the iceberg of my hatred was impervious to thaw. My soul was frozen in permanent winter and the spring of forgiveness was out of reach, no matter how hard I tried and prayed. I still had to completely numb out just to be in the same room with her. Even her breathing irritated me. I visualized bending her oxygen hose in half to halt the air flow. I sometimes imagined taking a sledgehammer and smashing the whirring oxygen concentrator into a million pieces. Sometimes, I felt like my imagining how many ways I could kill her was the only thing that stopped me from actually doing so.

I'd been working on myself for about eight years when I got to Memphis, and hadn't had a drink in six years. But it seemed as though all the progress that I'd made quickly unraveled living near my mother. It's one thing to sit across from a therapist and talk about your mommy issues. It's quite another when Mommy is pushing all your buttons. Mothers know exactly where every button is. They should, they installed them.

I schlepped back to therapy in sheer self-defense. This time, I found Robin, another tough-love therapist who didn't take an ounce of shit or self-pity. As I settled into the small love seat across from her, I thought idly that her hair and eyes were the same color of brown as my mother's – a few shades darker than that of a beer bottle. We sat in the tiny living room that also doubled as her office and I could hear her partner softly clanging some pots and pans, cooking dinner in the kitchen. I thought I smelled meatloaf, and although I'm not a fan of that type of thing, I was hungry and it did smell good. My stomach rumbled slightly in response. I ignored my growling stomach and jumped right into my current mama drama.

"She's driving me nuts. I think about killing her. She's just a fucking asshole like she's always been. All she thinks about is herself. She needs to sell that fucking house in Pennsylvania. It's just collecting dust and she needs the money. Her medical bills are piling up and she doesn't give a shit. My sister and I can't afford to pay for her shit," I whined.

"What is YOUR part in all of this?" Robin got right to the point.

"What the hell is *that* supposed to mean? Weren't you listening? She's driving me crazy! My part! What part do I have? I'm just here to help her and she's an ungrateful bitch! Don't you think it's weird that I want to kill her?" I hissed at her. I didn't want to raise my voice in her living room.

"You aren't a victim, you're a volunteer. No one forced you to come to Memphis. Your mother is and will continue to be the way that she's always been. It's totally up to you to decide how to respond. *You* make the choice how you want to react to her. She can only drive you crazy if you give her the keys."

She'd totally ignored my threat of matricide. Weren't therapists supposed to take that shit seriously? I threw consideration to the wind and shouted, "You don't understand! I don't have a choice!" I wanted to continue my throwing spree by tossing something at Robin. What the hell was wrong with people? Couldn't they see how my mother was treating me? How she'd always treated me? Whose side was Robin on? What in the hell was I paying this bitch for?

"YOU don't understand. You always have a choice in your response. Maybe that's one of your lessons here. No one chooses your reactions for you, it is always up to you," Robin said calmly.

Perhaps it would have been easier to deal with Trudy if she would have been grateful (or, at the very least, civil). But she had managed to elevate stubbornness and helplessness to new heights, or depths. Although she could get up and walk, she often refused to. She made it to the bathroom and back. She expected everything else to be delivered to the couch and every meal became a battle of wills.

"You need to get up and walk around. Why don't you go into the kitchen and get some lunch?" I sat in the rocking chair, unsuccessfully trying to hide my annoyance.

"You do it," the Imp commanded petulantly from the couch.

"No. You need to do it," I said firmly. My voice sounded far calmer than I felt.

"You do it," she repeated. A two-year-old couldn't have sounded more like a broken record.

"Well, when you get hungry enough, you'll get up and have lunch."

"I can't get up and I would like a tuna sandwich. You do it."

We stared at each other, yet another Mexican standoff.

When she couldn't connive anyone to wait on her, there was hell to pay. She constantly picked fights with five year old Michael and could give fifteen year old Alison the silent treatment for months. To say that she was not an easy person to love, let alone like, would be an understatement. Beth had the patience of a saint with her. I didn't have Beth's patience, but thanks to Robin's counsel, I somehow managed to not lose my temper with her. Always professional, I felt and showed no emotion toward her whatsoever, completely spaced out.

After a while, Beth and I fell into a routine. She cared for my mother's daily and medical needs and I was the business manager and enforcer. With an older sister's propensity for bossiness and nagging, it was my job to get my mother to meet her financial obligations. If she'd been frugal before her illness, Trudy became downright cheap on Beth's dime. She'd wait until the last minute to pay her bills or outright refuse to pay. She'd originally agreed to pay Beth a few hundred dollars a month, all of which would go toward food and the increased electric bill from the oxygen machine. Month after month, she would either "forget" to give Beth a check, or crying poor mouth, give her only a hundred dollars. It became my job to shake my mother down for the balance. After a year or so, my sister and I were long tired of my mother's money game. Beth finally put her foot down and refused to pay the electric bill. She told Trudy that she couldn't afford to pay the power bill and it would be my mother's responsibility to see that it got paid.

Trudy's response was predictable: "You do it."

My office phone rang and I was surprised to hear my mother's voice on the other end of the line. She never called me. I didn't even know that she knew my work number.

"Hi, it's me," Trudy's trembling voice sounded as close to panic as I'd ever heard.

"I'm obviously at work and can't talk, so please get to the point. What do you need?"

"The electricity is going to be shut off tomorrow if the bill isn't paid. Beth got the final notice in the mail today."

"Then give her a check for the bill. What's the problem?" My head started throbbing and I leaned my forehead against the cool glass of my computer monitor.

"Beth is supposed to pay the bill, not me," she whined.

"Well, if the power gets shut off, Beth and the kids will continue to breathe just fine. You, on the other hand, will not." I took a deep breath and held it so that I wouldn't start screaming in my cubicle.

She was silent for a minute. It seemed as though she hadn't considered that aspect of the situation. I waited silently while it sunk in.

"Beth has to work tomorrow. Will you come and get the check tonight and take it to Memphis LG&W first thing in the morning?"

"Yes. Have it ready after dinner." I hung up.

Picking the phone back up, I called Beth at work. "You finally won a round of chicken."

We both laughed a little, the kind of nervous giggle that people have right before they start screaming and can't stop. Had my sister and I known that our life would go on like that for three more years, I'm sure that one or both of us would have had a breakdown. For over a thousand days, every day brought some new issue with Trudy. Day in and day out, it became TMS: Typical Mama Sheeit. As her COPD progressed, Trudy was increasingly absent from Beth's sofa. Instead, she rotated in and out of hospitals and rehabs. Beth and I took turns being the squeaky wheel for her care, ensuring that her bed and room were clean and that she was getting the medical attention that she needed. We took turns visiting on alternate days so that neither one of us would get burnt out. Since my mother's drunken rages had alienated any other family members who might be inclined to visit, the burden of my mother's care fell solely on the shoulders of my sister and me. It never occurred to either one of us not to stand up for Trudy's care. In situations like this, people are often faced with a choice: we can do the right thing or we can do the easy thing. The two rarely go hand in hand. The easy thing to do would have been to ignore Trudy. After all, she probably would have ignored us. Neither my sister nor I are saints nor the martyr type, but we knew what the right thing was and we did it. I'm not sure how we did it. I suspect that God's grace had more than a little to do with it, as my altruism didn't make one bit of sense – even to me.

Doing the right thing was not without consequence. Although I was a complete automaton around my mother, the ordeal still took its toll on my personal life. I wasn't drinking, but for all the lack of emotional stability I had, I may as well have been. I took my frustration with my mother out on everyone around me, except for my coworkers. I screamed at Robin every week, got into numerous road rage incidents, and was irritable with Beth. I had one brief relationship that was so volatile that it was a wonder that we didn't kill each other. My needle bounced between numbness and rage; there was no middle ground. I felt like an animal in a trap and began to think of suicide again. How in the hell could my mother hang on so long? Why was God doing this to me?

Then, in the summer of 2001, my mother had a stroke. She'd survived many health crises already, and there was no reason to think that this one would be any different. At the rate things were going, I was sure that she was going to outlive me. After the rehab called to say that Trudy was on her way to the emergency room, I left work and got to the hospital just in time to meet the ambulance at the door of the ER. As the attendants backed her stretcher out of the vehicle, I looked down into Trudy's eyes and saw sheer panic for the first time ever. After forty-six years of battle, I finally had one moment of connection with my mother. I finally felt just a shred of compassion for her, and at that moment, a small, tiny piece of ice melted off of the glacier of my soul. Intuitively, I knew that it was beginning of the end. By the time that Beth arrived shortly afterwards, Trudy had already fallen into a coma. I told Beth about the terror that I saw in my mother's eyes and we resolved that she wouldn't be by herself when the end came. So my sister and I took turns sitting with her around the clock for the next three days. Left to my own devices, it wasn't something that I would have chosen to do, but it was another thing that I knew that I was supposed to do.

The nurses told us that people in comas can still hear, so during my time with her, I said everything to my mother that I'd ever wanted to say. To my surprise, the things that came out of my mouth weren't the things that I would have predicted. I'd always thought that I would say that I hated her and that I hoped that she would rot in hell. I thought that I would tell her to go fuck herself and that I hoped that she would encounter every demon in Satan's stable.

But to my surprise, that wasn't what came out at all. In the silence of the dark hospital room, I told my mother that I was sorry that our family had turned out the way that it had. I said that I knew that she'd had a hard life. I held her hand and apologized for the times that I was an ass. I reflected on our family and all of the things that had transpired over the years. I thought about the alcoholism and rage that we shared and told her that I thought that we'd both done the best we could under the circumstances. Sitting next to her bed, I read the Bible and prayed the Rosary. In the end, I told her that I loved her and that I forgave her. I held her hand as she passed away. As I watched her last breath, a huge weight lifted from my shoulders. I breathed a sigh of relief and sadness. The Imp was gone, but so was my mother.

It occurred to me years later that those three years with my mother had been a gift, as had her final three days. Although the struggle was long and hard, it enabled me to do much of the hard work that was required to become a different person. To become the type of person that would not end up in the same situation that my mother had, which was really what I had wanted from as far back as I could remember. I wanted to be who she wasn't. In those three years, I had changed more than I had realized. The proof was at the end, when I had to tell my mother everything I ever wanted to say, when no one else was around and she was completely powerless. The time when what came out was far different than what I intended to say. The time when the spring of forgiveness began to thaw the frigidity of my soul. And, at the end of the day, the time when my mother, in her own manner, lit my way to the exit of the dark house.

EPILOGUE

It seems obvious to the most casual observer that both of my parents were broken by generations of domestic abuse and alcoholism, but it is only obvious from the outside or from the perspective of time. Even through years of therapy and reflection, I discarded that observation, as it seemed as though there had to be something *else*, something really significant that destroyed them. The insanity had become normalized.

I think that my mother fell in love with an abuser and never really came to terms with that. Like many women, she thought she could change him. As evidenced by Bumpy's sudden rage against my sister, my mother was no stranger to domestic violence. But I still somehow believe that she started out as a kind person, as I had, and that the systematic violence inflicted by my father broke her. In turn, she then became a systematic abuser. To put it in simplistic terms, the violence made us mean.

Today, the wounds have healed into scars, but it wasn't luck that healed me, it was a lot of work. That's the good news for you, whatever your situation is. If it were luck, some would get better and some would stay broken. But if you're willing to do the work, you can also have the payoff; far better than lottery odds. I don't have all of the answers, but I have been able to identify five tools that worked for me: a belief in a loving God, sobriety, community, therapy, and forgiveness, in that order.

When I was broken, I couldn't heal myself no matter how hard I tried – and believe me, I gave it a mighty effort. I have come to believe that such abuse and trauma are the result of evil, whatever that might be. The only antidote for evil is God. I have no religion to push. Pick a belief or a God that works for you and go with it. If that one doesn't work, pick another. God hears our call. In turn, you will be called in the right direction. Some people wonder where God was when the abuse was occurring. I believe that God was there, but God wept. He doesn't interfere in our free will, but that doesn't mean that He is unaware of our suffering.

Next, you can't get well if you're using. Period. Nothing, nada, zip. While you're under the influence, it can't happen. Quit the shit. I also happen to believe that if you're an addict or alcoholic, evil is somehow called in while we're trashed. It's almost like a crack in your soul that acts as a homing device for the bad energy of the world. I felt it, and maybe you have too.

We can't heal in isolation. Human beings are hard-wired for community. Although I still believe I'm a loner in my heart, I know that's really just bullshit that I tell myself. I couldn't have survived my childhood by myself. My sister and I kept each other afloat in the sea of craziness, and my aunt and grandmother unknowingly did their part to help. Today, I have a partner, what's left of my family, friends, and my dogs. Even if you have nothing or no one, start with an animal. You may save each other.

For some reason, God can't or won't heal us while we're sitting at home on the couch watching Netflix. If you're as broken as I was, you'll also need professional help. I needed over thirty years of it, but it paid off. It seems as though God will do for us what we can't do for ourselves, but God won't do for us what we can do for ourselves. The important thing is to find a Sherpa to lead you out of the insanity. You wouldn't attempt to fix your car by yourself if the engine blew up, and you can't fix yourself, either.

Finally, the F word – forgiveness. I found that forgiveness is necessary, but it comes *after* the first four tools. We can't just make a decision to forgive and then go to the movies. It may be a long, slow, painful process if it's done right. I first thought the forgiveness is absolution, but it is not. It means that you are more important than anything else that has happened and that you will free your energy to love and live, not just exist in a cesspool of resentment and hate.

Every one of us has something that we have lived through or need to overcome. Your circumstances may be worse or better than mine, but every human being has *some* obstacle that no one can defeat on our behalf. The bad news is that you can't blame your future on anyone else, no matter how bad your past was or what your current circumstances are. The good news is that you can change so that your past doesn't become your future. As George Bernard Shaw said, "People are always blaming their circumstances for what they are. I don't believe in circumstances. The people who get on in this world are the people who get up and look for the circumstances they want, and if they can't find them, make them." If I can leave the dark house, anyone can. Although my struggle to overcome my past didn't end when my mother passed away, I have continued to overcome it and still do. In the process, life has become an adventure that I look forward to! I have been successfully successful for over twenty years, proving that my exit from the dark house is not an aberration. Freedom isn't free, but it *is* possible and *you* are the only who holds your own key.

ACKNOWLEDGEMENTS

Nothing worthwhile is ever done in isolation; the whole is always greater than the sum of its parts. Joy, thank you for my life, your love, and for showing me every day what true normal and happiness is. Thanks to the single member of my family that alcoholism left: Beth, I love and appreciate you more than you'll ever know. I'm very grateful to those who took time from their busy schedules to patiently and kindly review and improve on the early drafts of this book: Janet Hobbs, Rhonda Wardlaw, Marsha Pauley, Valerie Wood, Lisa Pederson, Beth Spinks and Alison Spinks. Special thanks to Carl and Ellie Augsburger of Creative Digital Studios, who took my rough idea and manuscript and transformed it into my dream!

RESOURCES

Alcoholics Anonymous
www.aa.org

Trauma Resolution Integration Program (TRIP) – Nova University
www.nova.edu/healthcare/clinics-services/psychology/trip.html

Family Violence Program – Nova University
www.nova.edu/healthcare/clinics-services/psychology/familyviolence.html

The Wellness Institute
www.wellness-institute.org

Florida Personal Growth Center
www.fpgcinc.com

Substance Abuse and Mental Health Services Administration
www.samhsa.gov

Childhelp: National Child Abuse Hotline
1-800-4-A-Child (1-800-422-4453)
www.childhelp.org

www.ingramcontent.com/pod-product-compliance
Lightning Source LLC
LaVergne TN
LVHW051234080426
835513LV00016B/1571
* 9 7 8 0 6 9 2 7 4 9 3 1 9 *